Publisher's warning:

You should always consult your baby's pediatrician before introducing new foods to your baby.

The recipes in this work feature "recommended" age indications from the age of 6 months +, that is to say when five months have passed since birth.

We remind you that introducing new food into a baby's diet must be carried out under the supervision of a pediatrician who is in a position to adapt nutritional diversification to each child, taking into account the possible risk of allergies.

The author and publisher cannot be held responsible if pediatric advice is not sought out before introducing a new ingredient to a child's diet. Remember that the most important criterium is caution; a baby is rarely a latecomer to nutritional diversification.

This work suggests soup recipes that you can serve with a spoon or in a bottle. If you opt to bottle feed soup, make sure the texture is liquid enough for your child to drink it easily.

For all further information, contact: the American Academy of Pediatrics (USA), the Royal College of Paediatrics (UK), Child Health (World Health Organization).

PREFACE

Nothing but happiness!

I am a cook. I am writing this book for my children Alphonse and Charlotte, and all other children, and for young mothers who all have the same desire and concern as me: giving their children the best market-fresh fruits, vegetables and ingredients, while at the same time introducing them to new tastes and smells from here or elsewhere.

Babycook is used to prepare the follow-up formula starting at 6 months, with fresh ingredients that keep most of their vitamins, minerals, and trace elements because they are steamed. But, as time went on, and especially with the rich variety of colors and smells available at the market, I wanted to move away from the more classic purées and compotes, and share with my children the pleasure of preparing and tasting "little entrées," which are quick and easy enough to prepare that they can be enjoyed every day. OK, but which ingredient should I choose and why? How should I cook it so that it brings happiness every time it's prepared?

I created these recipes in the same way that I devise my restaurant's menu: by season, with good ingredients from the market. Each recipe highlights the flavor of one product, sometimes seasoned with an herb, seasoning, or spice, or enhanced with a special pairing.

When the main ingredient is a vegetable (I love vegetables!), I have followed in Ducasse's foot-steps by playing with the "raw and cooked" and "crunchy and tender" nature of vegetables, to help children discover vegetables in many different forms as often as possible. I use playful presentation to help pique the child's curiosity and tempt him to nibble the bits on his plate or dip his finger in.

Of course, these discoveries must be made progressively. I designed Babycook Book recipes that will evolve as baby does, while respecting the rules of nutrition and giving directions that moms can adapt to their child's development, following each child's own rhythm. In each recipe I have indicated at what

babycook book

85 recipes from Chef Dad

New Edition

LES ÉDITIONS
Culinaires

age the dish is recommended. This age is only a guideline and should be verified with a pediatrician.

The tastes presented in these recipes will become richer and more refined as baby grows and develops. With time, you will be able to feed baby more precious ingredients: a green onion added to the vegetables in the steamer basket; young, raw spinach leaves added to the blender bowl to bring out a brighter color in a dish; a thin drizzle of olive oil; freshly chopped parsley to garnish a dish; or a few grains of fleur de sel to add taste.

The consistency of dishes will be modified when blending, depending on the number and length of the pulses, and the firmness of the product. The technique will not be the same for a cherry as it will be for a fava bean! It will also depend on the quantity of sauce, water, milk, or crème fraîche added to the ingredients between pulses. We will start with a velouté or soup that is thin enough to be drunk from a bottle. Then, we'll move on to a thin purée for babies just starting to eat with a spoon. Next, when baby starts to chew, we'll serve a purée with the consistency of "caviar," and finally we'll end with purées with small pieces that baby will eat when some teeth have come in.

The first chapter is a preview of the rest. It is dedicated to first experiences: the approach and mastery of the Babycook appliance; teaching mom about cooking baby's "meals"; and baby's likes and dislikes.

All of the recipes in the Babycook Book are presented with their Good pointss (according to cooks and nutritionists), and with my advice.

Now it's time for moms to take over and put their imaginations to work, because culinary diversity and food diversification go very well together…

David Rathgeber

Babycook Book's Chef Dad

CONTENTS

LITTLE BABY

First Meals
Ideas for Infants p.24

Red Lettuce Milk	26
Watercress Velouté	28
Carrot Soup	30
My First Artichoke	31
Winter Squash Velouté	32
Beet Purée	34
Kids' Compotes	36
Peach Pear	38
Strawberry Banana	39
Strawberry Pear	40
Apples and Cinnamon	41

BABY EVERY DAY

Baby day, every day

Done Fast, Done Well, Every Day p.42

Potatoshow : 44
French Style Mashed Potatoes 44
Potato Potage 46
Crème Vichyssoise 47
Cod Petals and Fork-smashed Zucchini 48
Cod Petals and Broccoli Buds 50
Rosemary Chickpea Purée 51
Free-Range Chicken Breast with Broccoli 52
Cream of Chicken 54
Button Mushroom Purée 55
Mousse of Avocado and Shrimp 56
Greek yogurt and herbs 58

Pop's Pasta: 60
Sliced Ham, Comté, au Jus 60
Tomato and Goat Cheese 62
Pesto 63
Spinach-Mozzarella Tagliatelli Nests 64

SUNNY DAYS

Sunny Days
Meals for Summer and Springtime p.66

Babaganoush 68
Tomato Fondue "Our Way" 69
Tomato Two Times 70
Melon Ball Soup 72
Mom and Baby, Two Peas in a Pod 74
Thyme for Green Bean Purée 76
Spring Velouté 77
Green Asparagus Velouté 78
Egg-Cellent Caponata 80
Quail's Egg à la Basquaise 82
Boiled Egg and Snow Peas 84
Andalusian Gazpacho 86
Zucchini Flan-tastic 88
Artichokes, Leaf by Leaf 90
Four Seasons of Purées and Casseroles 92

BABY COLD DAY

Dishes for Fall and Winter p. 98

Lentil and Dry-Cured Ham Velouté 100
Mom's Little Ham 102
White Bean Soup 103
Cauliflower Curry in a Hurry 104
Fava Bean Velouté 106
Cream of Spinach 107
Lets Dive into Endives 108
Mini Filet of Beef and Pan-Fried Potatoes 110

Exotic Tastes: 112
Pytt-i-Panna 112
Swedish Meatballs 114
My First Couscous 116
Mary Had a Little Lamb (Kefta) 118

BABY HAPPY DAYS

Meals for Special Days p.120

Scallop Tartare 122
Beef Stroganoff 124
Sea Bass with Dill 126
Fish Dumplings in Mushroom Sauce 128
Veal Cakes 130
Socca Niçoise 132
Tom, Tom the Turkey 134
Ham and Pumpkin Au Gratin 135
Ricotta Gnocchi 136
Heart and Sole 138
Swiss Chard au Gratin 140
Salmon Brandade with Swiss Chard 142

SWEETS FOR BABY

Desserts, Snacks, Teatime p.144

Yogurt Shakes à la Carte (5) 146
Langues de Chat 152
Banana Yogurt with Honey 154
Cherry Granité 155
Watermelon Granité 156
Strawberry Rhubarb Crumble 158
Fromage Blanc with Walnuts 160
Madeleines 162
Quince Compote 164
Vanilla Peach Compote 165
Cinnamini Cookies (Pepparkakor) 166
Chocolate Cookies 168
Mango Hedgehog and Marmalade 170
Cherry Clafouti 172
Candlemas Crêpes 174
Pancakes à l'orange 176

AT THE TABLE

Here we are. The little guy is 5 months old. He is about to start his exploration of the big, wide world by starting with the most essential part: how life tastes. And life, for the time being, with the exception of mom's arms and Dad's tickles, consists of the contents of his bottle. Cereals, simple compotes, and soups will give him a first taste, and prepare him for the transition from heart-to-heart to face-to-face, for the tender dialogue that baby's meals will become.

As a newborn, he knew how to breast-feed. He could recognize sweet, salty, acidic, and bitter tastes. Now it's time for him to refine those sensations and give his opinion of these discoveries with the facial expressions at his disposal. And if he doesn't like something? Don't force him. You can have him taste it a few days later, and then again… And if he still doesn't like it? Then that just means he has a personality and his tastes are asserting themselves!

Now he's a little bit bigger. He feels his bottle, and picks up and sucks on everything he can get his hands on. At around 6 months, he learns to open his little beak for a spoon, without pushing it away with his tongue. And at around 7 months, he can drink from "his" cup. Soon he will smile his first toothy grin. And at around 8 months, he'll transition from his bouncy chair to a highchair to be in a better position when mom, with her Babycook at her side, rings the dinner bell…

…and no one likes to wait when his tummy is rumbling!

Now it's time to introduce a new "salty" snack (which actually should not be salty at all, or barely, before the age of one, and only slightly even then!) or a different texture, because, after all, baby is eating less puréed foods than before and will soon, with the arrival of molars, be able to eat mini-bites of whole food, between 12 and 18 months.

Mom, who knows what we like, has set the highchair with baby's colorful dishes, decorated with designs that he will discover with delight little by little after each bite of this newfound flavor. Isn't that what mom had him taste a tiny spoonful of last week, to see if he liked it? Or to see if he might have an allergic reaction? Or maybe for both reasons.

Sometimes, she makes a pretty design with the purée. He puts his fingers in it (she always washes them before dinner time) and picks out little pieces. She laughs and says, “Don’t worry, you’re wearing your long-sleeved bib.” She tells stories about what is on his plate. He answers her and she pretends to understand. That’s how the conversation goes.

Don’t bother bringing toys to the table. They’ll only distract him, and what a pity that would be! Anyway, the food on his plate is quickly finished, without mom even having to insist, because she has perfectly calculated the portions. And if he’s still hungry, she’s sure to be able to find a piece of cheese.

The best time is market time, almost every day, “so we only eat the freshest produce,” says mom. Wide-eyed, we look at all the piles of colors, breathe in the smells, taste the samples that the merchants give to mom and baby (and Dad, too, on Sundays) when she asks for their advice. Because mom only wants “young, seasonal vegetables,” “ripe fruit,” “farm-fresh eggs,” “fish right out of the water” (she asks the fishmonger to “bone it”), and “tender meat” that she has the butcher grind right before her eyes

No time for dilly-dallying! Mom wants to put our purchases away quickly, so as to “not to break the cold chain.” Mom puts the frozen foods right into the freezer, right next to the little dishes that she freezes for baby (in individual portions) when she cooks them beforehand because he really likes them or because the vegetable is really big (like a pumpkin, for example!) and the whole family can enjoy it.

She wraps everything with plastic wrap before placing it in the refrigerator so that “the smells don’t mix together.”

And finally, she places the fruit, melons, etc., in separate baskets on the table, making sure they don’t touch. Mom knows that fruit containing water should never be put in the refrigerator, so as not to “ruin” their smell. Anyway, they won’t have time to bruise because we will have eaten them by the day after tomorrow.

But it’s when mom is preparing baby’s dinner (at the last moment) that we are the most attentive. She gets out “her” Babycook appliance and “her” Babycook Book (those two are always hanging out together).

And our mouths start watering…

Chef Dad's MARKET

Almonds.
Powdered starting at age 3. Whole starting at age 4, but not before so as to avoid swallowing down the "wrong tube," even if they are rich in fat, protein, minerals (calcium, magnesium, etc.), trace elements (manganese), vitamins (E and B9), and fiber.

Apple.
Valuable from 5 months old because they are rich in water, sugar, vitamin C (the Reinette reigns over this category), balanced micronutrients, and soft fiber (pectin). Choose ones that are firm and shiny (but not waxed). If eaten raw, cut immediately before serving, or sprinkle the pieces with lemon juice so that they do not turn brown.

Apricot.
A golden-colored fruit (carotene) with sweet flesh (carbohydrate) and soft fibers (facilitating passage through the intestines). Rich in potassium. Baby can start enjoying this fruit at 5-6 months old. Apricots do not ripen after picking.

Artichoke.
Full of minerals (potassium, calcium) and carotene. Artichokes contain insulin, which helps the body to assimilate minerals and keeps the intestinal flora in balance. Babies under 6 months should not eat them because of their high fiber content.

Asparagus.
This natural diuretic is tender and loaded with vitamins (C, B9, carotene) and minerals. Grown in the great outdoors, green asparagus has more taste than its white relative. It can be found in markets from mid-February to the end of June. Store it raw in a bunch for up to 4 days in the refrigerator, wrapped in a damp cloth or newspaper, with the points up. From 1 year old.

Avocado.
Imported from Israel, Florida, and South America all year round. Buy medium ripe, or when it gives a little when lightly touched (without pressing too hard, to avoid bruising). Let ripen at room temperature for a few days. The only fatty fruit, it's high in potassium, and especially essential fatty acids and vitamin E. Not to be eaten before 1 year old because a child's digestive system cannot handle it before then. Prepare it immediately before serving. Sprinkle with lemon juice so the flesh doesn't turn brown.

Banana.
As sweet (and nourishing) as it is yellow and spotted. Let ripen at room temperature because this tropical fruit does not like the cold! This fruit is full of potassium, magnesium, vitamin B, starch, and soft fibers. Baby's intestines can handle it at 5-6 months.

Basil.
Herb with tender branches and sweet leaves. Always used fresh. The base for pesto.

Bay Leaf.
An aromatic leaf often used in small quantities along with thyme. Remove from dish before serving.

Beef.
Steak from 8 months. Rich in protein, iron, zinc, and vitamins B1 and B2. Have the butcher grind it in front of you, and then serve it to your child within 3 hours.

Beets.
Well-liked when cooked because they are very sweet (sucrose), beets can also be enjoyed raw from 1 year old.

Blackcurrent.
Gives the kiwi a run for its money in vitamin C and calcium content. Perfect for baby starting at 1 year.

Boiled Ham.
As rich in protein, iron, potassium, and calories as red meat. For babies over 7 months old, as long as it is boiled, lean (or extra lean), and of high quality (off the bone, for example).

Broccoli.
The number 1 vegetable in vitamin C and calcium. Recommended from 5-6 months on. Choose one at the market with small, tightly closed buds between May and November. Light, easily digestible, and with soft fibers, broccoli goes well with salmon (starting at age 1) and other soft-fleshed fish.

Button Mushrooms.
Very rich in mineral salts (potassium!), trace elements, and vitamins B, D and K. Choose young, white mushrooms with no dark spots. Good for babies over 1 year old. Wait until your baby is 18 months old before feeding him Asian mushrooms.

Cabbage.
Can be found at the market all year round. Rich in vitamin C. Not to be given to baby before at least 18 months because its high fiber and sulfur content make it hard for little stomachs to digest.

Carrot.
When cooked, this vegetable is good for baby starting at 5-6 months if it is organic or from your garden (to avoid too many nitrates in the cooking water). Not to be served raw (grated) until baby is 2 years old. Buy “new carrots” from the end of April till the end of July, and “in season” carrots until mid-December. New carrots should be crispy and colorful, with fresh greens on top, and can be kept for several days in the refrigerator without losing their carotene content. They contain fiber that helps intestinal transit.

Cauliflower.
Tender, with a good dose of micronutrients and fiber (cellulose). Good for 18 months and older.

Celery.
Both celery root and celery stalks are rich in cellulose. Can be eaten at 8-10 months.

Cherry.
With their fructose and vitamin C, minerals, trace elements and soft fibers, cherries can be used in a compote starting at 1 year old (but without the pit until 4 years old). Cherries are fragile and spoil quickly when left out, however they contain too much water to be kept in the refrigerator. Get cherries that are not too ripe, but that are shiny, but still with good color, and with green stems and eat them within 48 hours after picking.

Chervil.
Carotene, vitamins C and K, calcium and potassium. Baby can eat this fairly young, always blanched.

Chestnut and Sweet Chestnut.
Both fruit of the chestnut tree (the chestnut tree’s bur contains several nuts; the sweet chesnut’s does not). Rich in carbohydrates. Not before 18 months.

Chicken (Breast).
Skinless! Light and easily digestible starting at 7 months. Lean and full of protein, with a good amount of iron, potassium, phosphorus, and B vitamins.

Chickpeas.
Nutritious and calorie-filled. Packed with vitamins, minerals, and trace elements. Should not be given to babies under 18 months because of the fiber and sulfur content. An ingredient in hummus, falafel and couscous. Choose them white, without wrinkles. Soak them overnight before cooking.

Chives.
Herb loaded with vitamin C, calcium, and magnesium. To be tried at around 1 year old.

Chocolate.
Toning (iron), energizing (calories), strengthens the immune system and nerve equilibrium (magnesium, potassium). Starting at 18 months.

Cinnamon.
Sweet spice for babies over the age of 1. A stimulant and antiseptic that helps when baby's tummy hurts.

Cod.
The leanest fish and one of the richest in potassium. Thin and firm, its flesh separates into "petals" after cooking. Good for baby starting at 7 months.

Coriander.
Lemony spice, in seed or powder form.

Couscous Semolina.
Carbohydrates and protein. After 8 months (because of possible gluten allergies). When cooked, it absorbs 3 times its weight in water.

Cucumber.
A cousin of zucchini, gherkins, and melons. A thirst-quencher and diuretic because it is rich in water. A good source of vitamins and minerals (including all the B vitamins). Choose small ones that are dark green, with a smooth, tight skin, because there will be less seeds and the fiber will be easier for baby to digest: cooked after 8 months, raw after 2 years.

Dill.
A hollow-stemmed plant, dill has a stimulating, antiseptic, diuretic, and anti-inflammatory effect.

Eggplant.
This cousin of the tomato contains potassium, carotene, and fiber. Choose one with smooth, tight, and very shiny skin, a uniform color and a fresh, green stem. Can be eaten starting at 1 year old.

Eggs.
Buy them "farm fresh," "organic", or "free range." The yolk is good for babies over 7 months (serve carefully to test for possible allergies), whereas whites should not be served before 12 months (both of them always hard-boiled). Soft-boiled eggs, fried eggs and omelets starting at 2 years. The yolk is better for baby because it is extremely rich in phosphorus, calcium, iron, iodine, and vitamins A, D, E, and B9. And let's not forget protein, fat and calories.

Endive.
Easily digestible both raw and cooked. Soft fibers. Good for babies over 1 year. Rich in water, minerals (potassium, calcium), trace elements (selenium), and vitamin B9.

Fava Bean.
Rich in protein, fat, and fiber, and loaded with iron and copper (which the liver uses to incorporate iron into the blood). Buy them when they are young and tender in the spring. Peel the skin under the pod off so that they will be tender and easily digestible after cooking. For babies over 14 or 15 months.

Fennel, or Sweet Dill.
This Mediterranean anis-flavored leaf vegetable is one of the richest fresh vegetables in water and sodium, and has a good amount of vitamins (A, B9, and especially C). Not before 1 year.

Fig.
Rich in calcium and fiber (pectin). Choose soft figs with firm stems. For children over 3.

Flat-Leaf Parsley.
Extremely good for your health! Flavor baby's soup and purées with parsley juice and, later on, with finely chopped leaves. This way baby will be able to enjoy the herb fresh, with its richness intact (potassium, calcium, magnesium, and vitamins C and K).

Fromage Blanc.
The dairy product that is richest in protein. Gives yogurt a run for its money in terms of calcium and calories. For babies over the age of 1.

Garlic.
Rich in nutritional value. An antioxidant and a germ and allergy fighter. New garlic, without its germ, is easily digestible.

Ginger.
This root is loaded with good qualities. It aids digestion, improves vision, and relieves respiratory problems. And as an infusion, it fights coughs, the flu, and nausea.

Grapes.
The sweetest fresh fruit. Full of minerals (potassium) and rich in fiber. Give seedless, skinless grapes to baby from 5-6 months. With seeds from 4 years.

Grapeseed Oil.
This oil is sweet and carries no risk of allergic reaction. Starting at 5-6 months old.

Green Beans.
Light and easily digestible. Full of minerals (calcium) and vitamins (B9, carotene). Rich in fiber. For babies over 5-6 months. Choose very thin beans.

Honey.
Contains sugar, of course, but also a good dose of iron, vitamins and micronutrients. Make sure to buy a pot with the name of the floral source and/or the region where it was produced. Acacia honey, which is clear and thin, is the sweetest variety. Not before 1 year and in very small quantities.

Kiwi.
Starting at about 8 months old. You know this fruit is loaded with vitamin C, but don't forget about calcium and iron, too! You can buy them firm and then ripen them next to an apple (farmer's tip).

Lamb.
A tender meat (protein, vitamin B, phosphorus, and especially iron!). Baby can enjoy it at 8 months old.

Leek.
A winter staple. But spring leeks, which are fragrant and delicate, are better for children (from 5-6 months). To be eaten often for its minerals, fiber, carbohydrates, vitamins, and diuretic effect. Choose them very fresh, long, straight, and white. The green tops should be straight and very green, even if we only give the white part to baby. Can be kept raw in the refrigerator for several days. Does not keep well cooked.

Lemon.
Vitamin C and calcium. Use lemon juice to keep avocados, mushrooms and apples from turning brown. Put a fewdrops in compotes every once in a while to help baby get used to the acidity.

Lentils.
Has important qualities. Rich in protein, carbohydrates and vitamins; high in iron, just like spinach; a lot of easily digestible fiber (but very little cellulose), which makes them good for babies 18 months and older. Choose French green lentils. Buy them dry, and soak them overnight before cooking for a long time, or buy them cooked and vacuum-packed.

Mango.
Choose one that is spotless and firm but which gives when you press on it. The color, which ranges from green to orange, specifies the variety and not the fruit's ripeness. For babies over 1 year, above all for its vitamin C and carotene.

Maple Syrup.
Canadian "honey".

Melon.
Hydrates, revitalizes, and acts as a diuretic. Rich in water, potassium, sugar, vitamins (C, carotene), and a whole rage of minerals and trace elements. Starting at 1 year, well-mashed.

Mint.
A fresh-smelling perennial. Soothing, antispasmodic, aids digestion.

Mozzarella.
Fresh, soft cheese from southern Italy, made with buffalo cow's milk. Rich in protein and lipids. The best comes from Italy's Campania region. For babies over the age of 1.

Nutmeg.
Sweet spice to be grated or used in powder form.

Oils: olive, corn, and sunflower
Preferably uncooked, for babies over 5-6 months. Peanut oil: not before 18 months (allergy risk). All of these are rich in calories, vitamin E, and essential fatty acids, which are good for baby's nervous system.

Onion.
Rich in carbohydrates, mineral salts, carotene, and B vitamins. This vegetable has antibacterial properties. Around 1 year.

Orange.
Starting at 5-6 months, for its vitamin C content, plus their carotene, vitamin B9, and soft fibers.

Papaya.
Famous in Tahiti for helping children to digest. Researchers sing its praises for helping to protect the body in other ways. Choose one that is soft. Not before 1 year.

Parmesan.
Among the cheeses the most rich in calcium and phosphorus. Starting at 8 months.

Passion Fruit.
Vitamin C and carotene. Choose one that is round and plump with smooth, shiny skin. For babies over 1 year.

Pasta.
Carbohydrates, protein, and calories. Baby can eat vermicelli or alphabet soup at 8 months and "grown-up pasta" at 10 months.

Peach.
One of the first fruits you can give to the little ones. One of the most fragile, as well. Thirst quenching, sweet, and full of vitamins (A) and soft fiber (if just ripe). Choose ones that are soft to the touch, but don't press so hard as to bruise them. Or buy them still slightly hard and let them ripen at room temperature away from other fruit. Prepare them immediately before serving.

Pear.
A summer, fall, and even winter fruit to be handled with care to avoid bruising. Cut it right before serving so that it doesn't turn brown. Refreshing and hydrating, this fruit contains soft fibers and several types of sugar, such as sorbitol, which stimulates digestion. Good for babies starting at 5-6 months. Continues to ripen after picking.

Peas "Fresh from the Garden".
From May to July in markets. Choose them smooth, shiny, plump, and fresh. Tender (soft fiber) and sweet (carbohydrates), these little treasures are the richest in protein of all the green vegetables. Fresh (organic) or frozen, babies can enjoy these in soups and purées from 10-12 months. But no whole peas before 3 years old to avoid swallowing down the "wrong tube"!

Pecan.
Very nutritious and full of calories. Rich in fatty acids, protein, minerals, trace elements, and vitamins (B1, B2, B3, and E). Good for babies over 3 years if ground very fine.

Petit Suisse.
A petit suisse cheese is equal to 60 ml of milk. From 7 months.

Pineapple.
One of the most vitamin-rich fruits. Stimulates digestion thanks to an enzyme called bromelain. Can be found fresh all year round. Choose one with very green leaves and an "air shipped" label, which guarantees that it was quickly transported from the tropics. Baby can start enjoying well-blended pineapple at 8 months.

Pine Nut.
Seed of the pine tree, whose subtle flavor has been enjoyed around the world since ancient times. Starting at age 3.

Pork.
Rich in Vitamin B, and especially B1. Use the breast meat to enrich a "big kid's" dish and the leaner cuts near 10 months. Wait as long as possible before charcuterie.

Potato.
When mashed with another vegetable, potatoes can be eaten around 7 months. Mashed with only potatoes around 8 months. Its richness in carbohydrates (such as starch) puts it far above other vegetables. And don't forget its wonderful variety of minerals and trace elements and its vitamin C content (that's right!). Best eaten freshly harvested starting in March ("new") until July 31st.

Quince.
The pectin in this fruit helps alleviate intestinal problems, just like carrots, but in recipes that are sweet (and cooked). Not before 8-10 months.

Raspberry.
Very fragile! Pick them yourself or buy them firm, fragrant, and with a frosted appearance. Enjoy this fruit, rich in vitamins A and C, and fiber, immediately after purchase. For babies over 1 year.

Red lettuce.
Colorful lettuce with tight leaves (tinged with red), a crunchy, firm center, and a sweet taste. This vegetable is rich in water, fiber, minerals, trace elements, and vitamins. Well cooked, after 5-6 months.

Rhubarb.
An astringent with plenty of dietary fiber. Wait until baby is 1 year old.

Ricotta.
Cheese made from goat or sheep's milk and an integral part of the traditional cuisine of Italy's Campania region. Used in many desserts, like the Pasteria at Easter from Naples.

Rice.
As rich in carbohydrates as pasta but gluten free. Preferably cooked in milk. After 8 months.

Rosemary.
Tonic and stimulating.

Sage.
A slightly bitter Mediterranean plant. Aids digestion and acts as a stimulant.

Salmon.
A migratory fish that is born in fresh-water, migrates to the ocean, and returns upstream in fresh water rivers to reproduce. Wild salmon less than 3 years old from Scotland and Scandinavia is a true delicacy. This "cold water fish" is rich in essential fatty acids and vitamins A and D, which help the body to assimilate the calcium and phosphorus it contains. Good for babies over the age of 8 months.

Salsify.
Carbohydrates, fibers. After 18 months.

Savory.
A sweet, citrus-scented Mediterranean plant.

Scallops.
Protein, vitamin C, phosphorus, iodine, and zinc. After 18 months.

Sea Bass.
It's called "Atlantic Sea Bass" when fished in Brittany but just a "sea bass" when it comes from the Mediterranean. A lean fish, rich in protein, iodine and fluoride. From 7 months.

Shallots.
The pink skinned variety has a sweeter taste. "New" shallots arrive in July. Choose firm shallots with tight skin the rest of the year. Not before 14/15 months.

Shrimp and other shellfish.
Protein, iodine, zinc, and vitamin C! Buy precooked (except when fresh from the sea), firm, and without a fishy smell. For children over 2.

Sole.
A lean white fish, very rich in calcium, phosphorus, iodine, and fluoride. Ideal for baby starting at 7 months. Buy it extremely fresh, and serve well-cooked.

Spinach.
High in iron, fiber, mineral salts (potassium, calcium and magnesium), trace elements (fluoride), and vitamins (C, K, B9). Spinach is safe for babies 5-6 months old if it is garden grown or organic. Otherwise, wait till baby is at least a year old (too many nitrates in the cooking water is not good for young babies). This leafy green can be found fresh all year round (although it does not withstand the summer heat very well). Choose young leaves that are fresh, tender, shiny, and deep green in color. Wash and keep in the refrigerator in a towel if raw, but eat immediately once cooked.

Strawberry.
Choose strawberries that are ripe and bright in color with no bruises. Eat them quickly, without placing them in the refrigerator or near other fruits. They are sweet (fructose) and have a balance of vitamins (C, carotene) and minerals. This fruit contains salicylic acid (aspirin, yes!), which is where it gets its medicinal properties. However, they do give off histamines, which is why some people are allergic to them. Introduce this sweet treat to baby's diet little by little starting at 1 year.

Sweet Pepper.
Choose the sweeter red ones rather than the green because they contain twice the vitamin C and carotene. Buy them firm, shiny, smooth, and without spots or bruises. At about 8 months in purée.

Swiss Chard.
Easy to grow in the kitchen garden, wonderful to eat. White stem and green leaves. This vegetable with soft fibers is rarely recognized for the carotene and vitamin C in its leaves; it also contains potassium, calcium and iron. From 10 months.

Tarragon.
A spice with small leaves and a slight anis flavor that comes out in cooking.

Thyme.
Usually used cooked. Choose a very fragrant variety with smaller leaves. Aids digestion.

Tomato.
Very ripe, seedless, and cooked tomato flesh is good for babies over 5-6 months, but raw tomatoes should not be eaten by babies under the age of 1. Wait until May to buy tomatoes at their peak in smell, taste, vitamins (a lot of vitamin C!), and minerals. Once bought, store them at room temperature. Cold air robs this red gem of its taste.

Turkey.
Protein, phosphorus, potassium, magnesium, and iron. This "chicken of India" was discovered by Christopher Columbus in North America. Babies over 7 months old can eat cutlets.

Turnip.
For potassium, calcium, carbohydrates and vitamins. A light little spring vegetable. Starting at 18 months.

Vanilla.
Sweet-smelling bean from the tropics whose seeds are prized for their delicious flavor.

Veal.
Lean and tender meat. Veal cutlets can be given to babies at 8 months.

Walnut Oil.
Strong taste, not before 18 months.

Walnuts and Hazelnuts.
To avoid swallowing down the "wrong tube," don't give these to children under 3, even in powder form and even though they are rich in lipids (essential fatty acids), protein, phosphorus and fiber. Fresh walnuts can be bought in the fall.

Watercress.
Tones and replenishes the body's minerals! With almost as much calcium and vitamin C as parsley, it is one of the richest vegetables in vitamins (B9, carotene) and minerals. Good for babies around 6 months old if it comes from a certified watercress bed that is watered with spring water. But please, no wild watercress, especially for baby!

Watermelon.
Dripping with water, rich in vitamins. Choose one with a rind that is smooth, thick, soft, and homogenous in color, with a small crack by the stem that says that it is ripe for the picking. Good for babies starting at 8 months.

White Bread.
The crust can be munched on at 10 months but the soft center not until 18 months. Whole-grain bread will have to wait a little longer: 7 years old, the age of reason. Carbohydrates, protein, vitamin B9, fiber, and gluten (watch out for allergies).

Wild Strawberry.
This ancestor of commercially grown varieties is very fragile. Make sure not to buy them over-ripe, bruised, or wet. And enjoy them right away. This fruit, rich in vitamins A and C, and fiber, is for babies over 1 year.

Wild Thyme.
Has a subtle flavor.

Winter Squash.
From 5-6 months. Extremely rich in potassium, with a very large amount of carotene. Like its cousin the pumpkin, this vegetable comes from the squash family from North America. How to identify it? By the stem and its flat top.

Yogurt.
Calcium! Fermented milk is valued for its protein and vitamins (B2, B12). Even better: special "just for baby" yogurts, which are made with enriched milk and are specially formulated for children from 7 months. Enriched in iron and essential fatty acids.

Zucchini.
Zucchini can be found today in markets from May to October. Choose a young, long, and skinny one that is firm, smooth, and uniform in color (dark green). They should be eaten within 48 hours after buying because they dry out very quickly. Light and easy to digest, with soft fibers and a good amount of vitamins and minerals. Good for baby starting at 5-6 months old.

DIETARY DIVERSIFICATION

With new foods come new flavors. But at what age?

Food diversification is in some ways a treasure hunt, a quest that all children experience. During this quest, they take advantage of their evolving abilities and explore the world - stealthily - for tastes and flavors. Don't worry about their caution; there are reasons for it. Curiosity will win them over in due course, if it is encouraged.

He is 5 months old. Breast milk and formula no longer provide enough calories to fuel his growth spurts. At 3 years old, his birth weight will be tripled, his sized doubled, and his brain will already have accomplished the majority of its development.

And yet his digestive system is still in the process of developing and will be for a bit longer. As time goes on, his stomach will be able to digest certain proteins (we choose them). His liver will reach maturity around the age of 3. Until then, he will only be able to digest fat in small amounts (we avoid them). His pancreas only produces a very small amount of insulin until the age of 6 months and then only slightly more until the age of 3, which barely stimulates the assimilation of sugars (we forget them for as long as possible), except for starch. His kidneys only start eliminating salt at 3 months (he barely needs any before the age of 1). His intestines are sensitive to everything except soft fibers (keep things soft!). And he will not have an immune barrier for several months after birth, so we stay away from foods that cause intolerances (gluten) and allergies (iodine, egg yolk, strawberries, etc.).

Each food has its good and bad qualities, except for breast milk, "nature's wonder food." Nevertheless, this food must be complemented and eventually replaced.

But no one food contains all of the nutrients necessary for a balanced diet of a quickly growing baby. And yet the body cannot produce all of the essential vitamins, minerals and trace elements that it needs every day.

So? A varied diet will be the best way to guarantee a healthy and fit body, as well as a good way to ensure happy taste buds, so long as parents start early and take the opportunity when baby is fascinated with discovering new things, because each new food is another addition to the range of familiar colors, smells and flavors. If parents wait too long, baby will become suspicious of the unknown and it will be too late to convince him to try everything. Take it slowly, though. Dinnertime must be a special time of the day. Shhhh! We're tasting!

When it comes to food diversification, each baby follows his or her own nose. The pediatricians' advice is there to guide moms. The contents of baby's bottle shows moms how big their baby's stomach is growing. And baby's reaction to food, his size-weight ratio, and his appetite for life show moms if baby is eating right. But the road ahead is still a guessing game.

But there is a common road map.

Basic until the age of 3: milk, always and forever, for its unique richness in animal proteins and calcium. If baby already has deficiencies in iron, calcium, etc., he is not eating a diverse enough diet. Absolute minimum: 1/2 liter per day after 6 months, including dairy products. But no cow's milk before 1 year old and then only in dairy product or cheese form until the age of 3. Milk is not easily digestible and is not rich enough in two very precious elements: iron (to oxygenate the red blood cells) and essential fatty acids (that help the brain to develop). So? Prepared baby formula from 4 to 12 months, and milk-based pediatric nutritional supplement from 1 to 3 years old. And that's it. And if possible, assorted "just for baby" dairy products.

Nourishing: Cereals and starches add their carbohydrates (starch among them) and their calories to the lactose. Special flours for infants can be used around 5 or 6 months (never before and always without gluten), in a bottle at first. Later, around 7 or 8 months, you can try potatoes, pastas and semolina in desserts and snacks.

Remineralizing and revitalizing: fresh fruits and vegetables, with soft fibers, starting at 5-6 months old. Cooked - no raw veggies before 2 years old. And in growing quantities that become fancier over time. For their vitamins, mineral salts, and trace elements, and for their water content, both thirst quenching and hydrating in summer.

Eggs can be eaten from 7 months, starting with half of a hard yolk. Wait until 12 months for half an egg with the white and 18 months for a whole egg, hard-boiled or in desserts. Soft-boiled eggs can be eaten from 2 years.

Full of vitamins: butter, starting at 4-6 months, raw, in small amounts (vitamins A and D). A little crème fraîche, the lightest of the fats, given to baby on the end of a teaspoon. Small drizzles of uncooked olive oil starting at 6 months (vitamin E and essential fatty acids).

Rich in protein: very lean poultry; boiled ham (without fat); and red or white meat, but lean! Starting at 7 months. Essential for the quality of their protein and iron, and easier for the body to assimilate. But in small portions until 3 years old (portions are usually 3 times too large!).

Full of iodine and fluoride, and as well as protein lean fish, starting at 7 months. To grow big and strong, with teeth for taking a bite out of life. The only fatty fish recommended is salmon, for its essential fatty acids and vitamin D, a vitamin that is crucial for the body's assimilation of calcium and phosphorus.

For everything else, we wait: 12 months for mozzarella, cinnamon, and chives; 15 months for fava beans and omelets; 18 months for cabbage, lentils and other dry legumes, and chocolate; at least 2 years for shrimp and shellfish; 3 years for figs, nuts, almonds, pinenuts, and chickpeas.

No need to rush. It's better to thoroughly explore the palette of flavors already at baby's disposal!

**Watch out for allergic reactions*

Diversification Table for 5 to 24 Months

AGE	5/6 mo.	7 mo.	8 mo.	10 mo.	12 mo.	14-15 mo.	18 mo.	24 mo.
Fruits								
Apricot, banana, orange, peach, pear, apple, plum, grape	X							
Pineapple, quince, kiwi, mango, watermelon			X					
Strawberries and berries*					X			
Exotic fruits, rhubarb					X			
Chestnut							X	
Vegetables								
Artichoke, beet, carrot, zucchini, broccoli florets, watercress, spinach, green bean, lettuce, leek, winter squash, red lettuce, tomato	X							
Asparagus, eggplant, avocado, button mushrooms, endive					X			
Swiss Chard, celery, peas				X				
Cooked cucumber, melon, sweet pepper			X					
Cabbage, cauliflower, legumes, turnip, salsify							X	
Frozen Spinach, fennel, onion					X			
Shallot, fava beans						X		
Pickles, crudités								X
Starches								
Cereals for infants	X							
Potato (mashed, with other vegetables)		X						
Mashed potatoes, pasta, rice, semolina			X					
Bread crust, crackers				X				
Bread (crust and white)							X	
Dairy								
Petit Suisse, yogurt		X						
Shredded semi-soft cheeses; soft cheeses			X					
Fats								
Butter, cream, oils (except for peanut and walnut oils)	X							
Peanut and walnut oil*							X	
Eggs*								
Yolk (hard-boiled)		X						
Whole egg, hard or well cooked-boiled					X			
Whole egg, soft-boiled								X
Fish								
Lean fish: cod, sea bass, sole		X						
Salmon and other fatty fish			X					
Scallops							X	
Shellfish								X
Meat								
Turkey, boiled ham, chicken		X						
Lamb, beef, veal			X					
Lean pork				X				
Sweets								
Honey*					X			
Chocolate							X	

LITTLE BABY

First Meals
Ideas for Infants

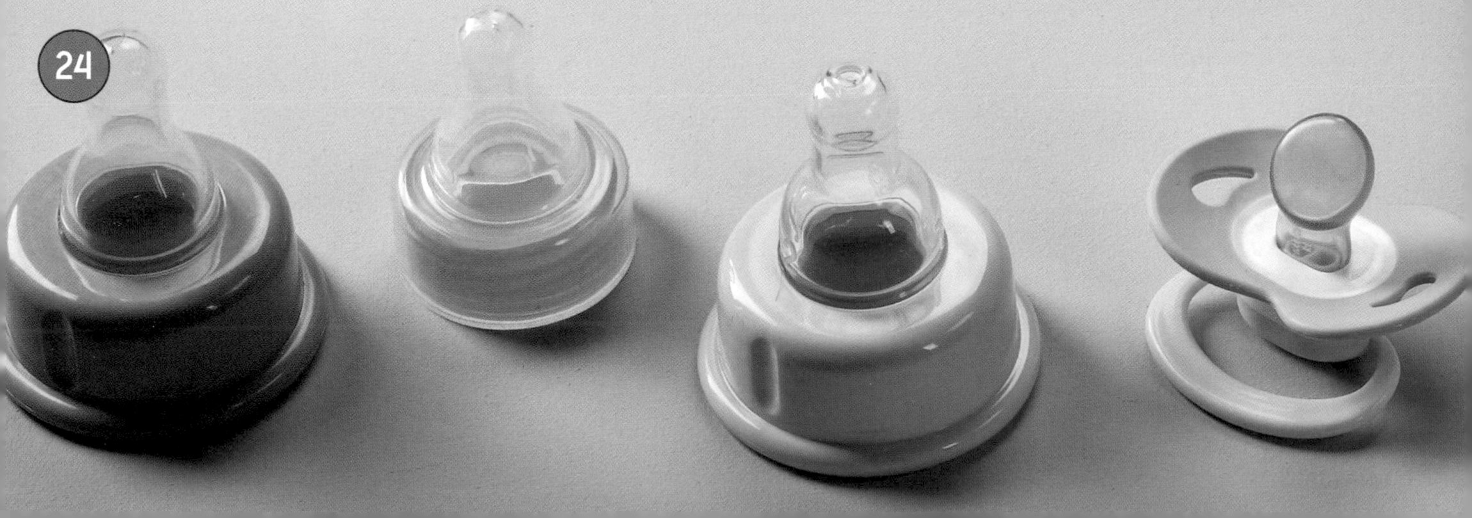

Red Lettuce Milk

Watercress Velouté

Carrot Soup

My First Artichoke

Winter Squash Velouté

Beet Purée

Kids' Compotes:

Peach Pear

Strawberry Banana

Strawberry Pear

Apples and Cinnamon

7 months and up | 15 mn

Red Lettuce Milk

… at the market: 1 head of red lettuce or mini head of green lettuce - 1 medium sized agria or charlotte potato - 1 sprig of chervil
… at the grocery store: 5 tbsp of follow-up formula for children under 12 months; prepared milk-based nutritional supplement for children over 12 mo.; 1 tbsp crème fraiche for older children.

cutting board - paring knife - scissors - dish towel

This recipe adapts watercress velouté for younger babies, and will remain on the menu for a long time: watercress velouté becames a more tender red lettuce or small green leaf lettuce milk.

Prepare the Lettuce: Throw the bigger leaves and core away. Keep only the lettuce heart. Wash the lettuce and the potato. Cut them into pieces. Wash again. Place in the steamer basket.

Cook for 10 min (water level 2). Wash and towel dry the chervil, and cut up with scissors.

Throw away the cooking juices. Transfer the vegetables to the blending bowl. Add the milk or formula (depending on the age of your child) and the cut chervil.
Blend: 2 to 3 pulses, depending on the desired consistency.
The mixture should be light and thin enough to be drunk from a baby bottle, if desired.

GOOD POINTS: *Red lettuce is a small leafy vegetable that is crunchy, sweet, rich in water, and stuffed with numerous micronutrients.*

7 months and up 15 mn

Watercress Velouté

... at the market: 1/2 bunch watercress - 1/2 baking potato
... at the grocery store: 1 Tbsp vinegar - 1 Tbsp prepared baby formula
...and for a 1 year old: take away the milk - add 1/4 white onion
large bowl - paring knife - vegetable peeler - cutting board - chinois

For little ones from 7 to 12 months: Soak the watercress, with the top of the bunch facing down, in a large bowl of vinegar water. Then rinse it several times in running water. Cut the tops off with a knife, leaving a little bit of the stem (1 inch). Thoroughly wash the potato, peel it with a vegetable peeler, and wash it again. Cut half of the potato into smaller pieces. Cook everything for 10 minutes (water level 2) in the steamer basket. Throw the cooking juices away.

Transfer the cooked vegetables to the blending bowl. Pulse 3 times. Add the milk before the 2nd pulse and a small amount of slightly mineralized water before the 3rd pulse if you desire a consistency that is thin enough to be drunk from a baby bottle.

For babies 1 year and up: Peel the onion. Chop 1/4 of the onion into small pieces and add them to the steamer basket and cook for 10 min.

When vegetables are cooked, transfer them to blending bowl, pulse 3 times. Add a small amount of slightly mineralized water (but no milk) between each pulse, to obtain a velouté. Strain the mixture through the Chinois to obtain a perfectly thin velouté.

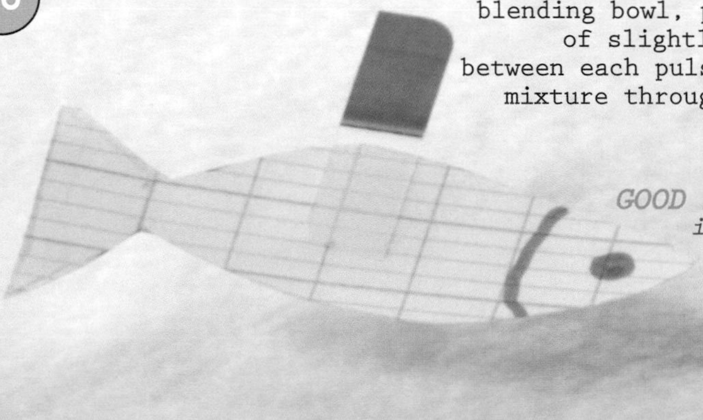

GOOD POINTS: Watercress is only to be eaten if it comes from a certified watercress bed that is watered with spring water. This is one of the vegetables richest in vitamins (B9 or folic acid, and carotene) and minerals (especially calcium).

7 months and up · 20 mn

Carrot Soup

… **at the market:** 1 carrot - 1 small Yukon Gold potato
… **at the grocery store:** 1 pat butter

cutting board - vegetable peeler - paring knife

For little ones from 7 months to 1 year: Thoroughly wash the carrot and potato. Peel them with the vegetable peeler and wash them again. Cut the carrot into small slices, dice the potato, and cook them for 15 minutes (water level 3) in the steamer basket. Throw the cooking juices away. Transfer the vegetables to the blending bowl. Pulse 3 times. Add a small amount of slightly mineralized water between each pulse, until you obtain a smooth consistency that is thin enough to be drunk from a baby bottle. Make it a bit thicker later on, when baby starts learning to eat from a spoon.

For babies over 1 year old: Forget about the potato! Prepare the carrots as above, but sprinkle them with a bit of salt before cooking them. Throw the cooking juices away and blend until you obtain the desired thin consistency. Pour the velouté into baby’s bowl. Cut the butter into little pieces and sprinkle it on the mixture, so baby will have the pleasure of seeing “little suns” melt on an orange-colored sky.

GOOD POINTS: *Carrots! For their bright color and sweet taste. The beta carotene they contain gives you beautiful skin and rosy cheeks (and a rosy bottom!), and their soft fibers aid digestion. Make sure to buy them straight from the garden or organic (so that they contain as few nitrates as possible). Potatoes add starch, minerals, and vitamins. And butter is an excellent source of A vitamins when eaten raw.*

6 months and up — 25 mn

My First Artichoke

… at the market: 1 artichoke - 1 Tbsp prepared baby formula

… at the grocery store: 1 drizzle olive oil instead of the prepared baby formula for infants over 8 months

cutting board - paring knife - teaspoon

For little ones from 6 to 8 months: Wash the artichoke under running water. Vigorously shake it off, with the head facing down. Peel off the first few leaves and break the stem by hand to pull out all of the artichoke's hard fibers. Cut the raw artichoke around the bottom. Remove the choke with a teaspoon and cut the heart into big chunks. Cook the pieces for 15 minutes (water level 3) in the steamer basket. Throw the cooking juices away. Transfer the pieces to the blending bowl. Pulse 3 times, adding a little milk between each pulse to obtain a velouté that is thin enough to be drunk from a bottle; or pulse only twice, and add a little milk or slightly mineralized water between pulses to obtain a purée that can be eaten with a spoon. Pulse only once for a "big kid's" purée with little chunks.

For little ones over 8 months: Mix by pulsing once without milk or water. Decorate the dish with a little drizzle of olive oil.

GOOD POINTS: *Artichokes are extremely rich in minerals. It also contains a type of sugar, insuline, which helps the body to assimilate these minerals, is good for a balanced intestinal flora, and gives the veggie its sweet taste, which is enjoyed even by very young children.*

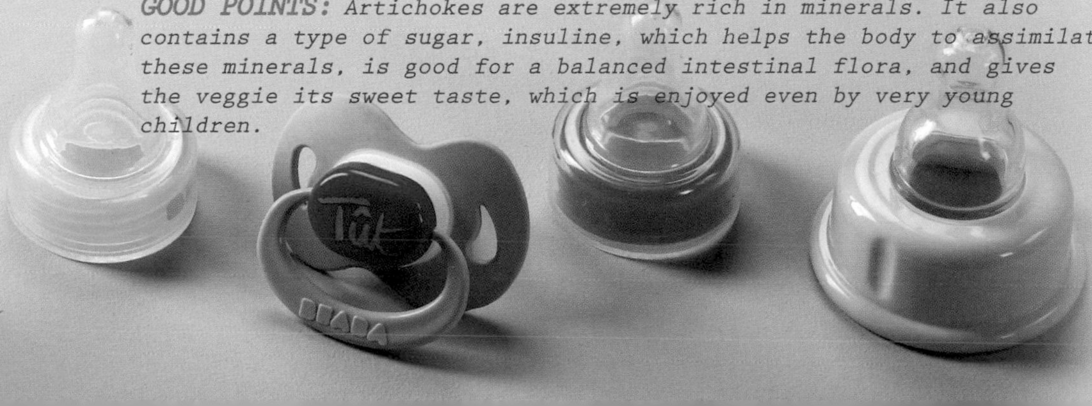

6 months and up · 20 à 25 mn

GOOD POINTS: *Tender and sweet, winter squash is recommended for babies from 5/6 months because of its abundance of potassium, iron, magnesium, soft fibers, and beta carotene, which gives it its sunny color. Egg yolk makes a good mate, with its high-quality proteins, phosphorus, and vitamin content (especially B vitamins).*

Winter squash Velouté

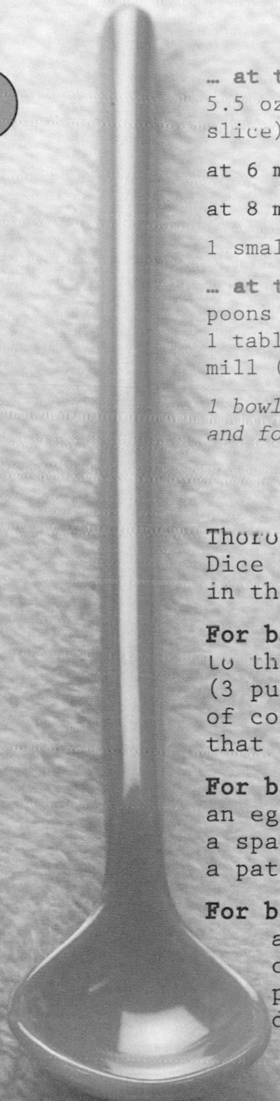

… at the market: 3.5 oz winter squash for a 6 month old - 5.5 oz winter squash for an 8 month old - 7 oz winter squash (= 1 large slice) for a 1 year old

at 6 months: 2 tablespoons prepared baby formula

at 8 months: 1 farm-fresh egg yolk from a free-range chicken

1 small pat butter

… at the grocery store: For children over 1 year only: add 2 tablespoons prepared milk-based pediatric nutritional supplement - 1 tablespoon olive oil - 1 tiny pinch salt - 1/4 turn of the pepper mill (white pepper)

1 bowl - tablespoon - cutting board - paring knife…
and for babies over 8 months: spatula - another bowl

Thoroughly wash the squash. Remove the rind and seeds. Dice the flesh and cook it for 15 minutes (water level 3) in the steamer basket. Pour the cooking juice into a bowl.

For babies 6 to 8 months old: Transfer the cooked flesh to the blending bowl. Add the milk. Blend the ingredients (3 pulses) to obtain a perfect velouté. If necessary, add a bit of cooking juice between pulses until you obtain a consistency that is thin enough to be drunk from a baby bottle.

For babies 8 to 12 months old: Before blending, add to the milk an egg yolk. Pulse twice, mixing with a spatula between pulses. Garnish with a pat of cold butter before serving.

For babies 1 year and up: Season the velouté with a bit of salt (and a very tiny bit of pepper for 2-3 year old children), pour it into a bowl, and decorate it with thin drizzle of olive oil.

6 months and up 10 mn

Beet Purée

… at the market: 1 cooked (or vacuum packed) beet
… at the grocery store: For young babies: pre-prepared formula

cutting board - paring knife - fork

Remove the skin from the cooked beet. Cut into pieces and place in the mixer.

Pulse twice, adding a little bit of milk between each pulse to obtain a smooth consistency that can be served in a bottle. For a purée that can be eaten with a spoon, use a little slightly mineralized water. For a chunkier purée for older babies, pulse only once without adding milk or water.

GOOD POINTS: *Red beets have a fine, sweet flavor that babies love. Beets were cultivated by Egyptians for their medicinal properties and are recommended for headaches and toothaches! Rich in vitamins B and C, magnesium, phosphorus and fiber…even its leaves, which taste like spinach, contain vitamin A, iron and calcium.*

6 months and up | 10 to 15 mn

Kids' Compotes

Down to Basics. Seasonal fruit mixes, to be made up immediately before feeding them to baby. To be served lukewarm, cool, or even chilled (for babies over 1). Add a little sugar, if need be, and keep the cooking juices in a cool place for snack time.

Kids' compotes

Peach-Pear Compote

… at the market: 2 nicely colored peaches - 1 Bartlett pear
… at the grocery store: A sprinkling of sugar

cutting board - paring knife - 2 large glasses (or bottles)

Thoroughly rinse the fruit. Peel the pear, cut it into four pieces, and remove the core and seeds. Cut the flesh into pieces and place them directly into the steamer basket. Peel the peaches by running the back edge of the paring knife over the skin of the peaches so that the skins come off easily, cut them in half, and pit them. Cut the flesh into pieces and place them in the steamer basket. Cook them for 5 minutes (water level 1). Keep the cooking juices in a glass to enjoy as a snack with for example, a langue de chat (see page 152), for babies over 8 months old. Transfer the fruit to the blending bowl and pulse once. Taste and, if necessary, sprinkle with a bit of sugar. Serve while still lukewarm.

GOOD POINTS: *Peaches and pears are perfect for little ones. They are refreshing, hydrating, light, and full of vitamins and soft fibers. And, in addition to the sugar found in peaches, the sorbitol in pears stimulates digestion. But both of these fruits are fragile, so handle them with care and prepare them at the last minute.*

6 months and up — 10 to 15 mn

Strawberry-Banana Compote

... at the market: 1/2 ripe banana

and for children over 1 year: 1/2 pint strawberries (1 cup whole berries)

... at the grocery store: *A sprinkling of sugar*

cutting board - paring knife - strainer - 2 large glasses or bottles

Peel the banana. Cut half of the banana into large pieces. Place them in the steamer basket. Rinse the strawberries in a strainer under running water. Then dry and stem them. Add them to the steamer basket. Cook everything for 10 minutes (water level 2).

Transfer the fruit to the blending bowl. Pulse 2 or 3 times to mix the fruit together. Add the cooking juices (in small quantities) between each pulse, until you obtain a light compote of the desired consistency. Save the cooking juices for a snack (for example, for children over 1 year, with a white or dark chocolate cookie from p. 168) Add a bit of sugar before serving if needed.

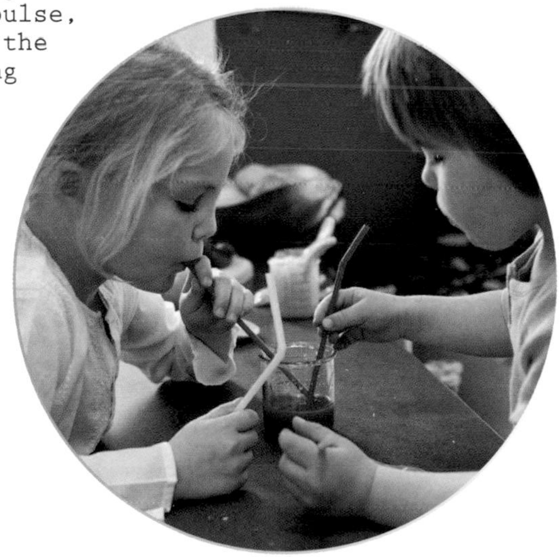

GOOD POINTS: *Dense, soft, and sweet, bananas are a wonderful source of potassium and magnesium. Light and revitalizing, strawberries are jam-packed with fructose and vitamin C - but don't forget to watch out for allergic reactions.*

12 months and up · 10 to 15 mn

Kids' compotes

Strawberry-Pear Compote

… at the market: 1/2 Comice or Bartlett pear
And after 1 year: 1/2 pint strawberries (1 cup whole berries)

… at the grocery store: A sprinkling of brown sugar

cutting board - paring knife - strainer - 2 large glasses or bottles

Wash and peel the pear, cut it into quarters and remove the core and the seeds. Place the quarters in the steamer basket. Rinse the strawberries in a strainer with cold water. Then dry and stem them. Add them to the steamer basket. Cook them for 10 minutes (water level 2). Keep the cooking juices in a glass to enjoy as a snack with for example, a madeleine (see page 162), for older babies. Transfer the fruit to the blending bowl and pulse twice to obtain a light and liquid compote.

Taste and carefully add sugar until the compote is flavorful, without overpowering the taste of the fruit.

GOOD POINTS: *Strawberries are chock-full of fructose and vitamin C when ripe. But the risk of allergies because of their histamine content requires parents to wait 1 year before introducing them slowly but surely into baby's diet. Pears are rich in water, sugar, and vitamins.*

MORE WAYS TO LOVE IT: *Bartletts are summer pears. They are juicy, savory and have a lovely scent. They are perfect for compotes and marmalades or smashed with a fork. Comice pears are spring pears and keep well.*

12 months and up — 10 to 15 mn

Apple-Cinnamon Compote

... at the market: 2 golden delicious apples
... at the grocery store: 1 sprinkling of brown sugar - 1 stick of cinnamon - a pinch of powdered cinnamon

cutting board - paring knife - strainer - 2 large glasses (or bottles)

Wash and peel the apples. Cut into quarters. Remove the core and seeds. Cut the quarters into small pieces and place in the steamer with the cinnamon stick. Cook for 15 min (water level 3).
Save the cooking juices in a glass. Remove the cinnamon stick. Transfer the fruit to the mixer. Pulse 2 or 3 times, adding a little of the cooking juices between each pulse until you obtain a light, fluffy compote. For thicker, chunkier compote, pulse only once. Sprinkle with brown sugar.

Taste and add a tiny bit of powdered cinnamon to enliven the flavor and the color.

GOOD POINTS: *An excellent recipe for autumn and winter. Cinnamon is one of the oldest known spices. It has an antiviral and stimulant effect. It is used to fight colds, flu and digestive problems.*
The savory, tender apple is a good source of calories with its fructose and carbohydrates. It supplies the body with vitamins and minerals and is very thirst quenching.

MORE WAYS TO LOVE IT: *Cut the apples into little pieces. Replace the cinnamon with a vanilla bean (which should be removed before mixing). Smash the apples with a fork right after they finish cooking.*

BABY EVERY DAY

Baby day, every day
Done Fast, Done Well, Every Day

Potatoshow :

French Style Mashed Potatoes

Potato Potage

Crème Vichyssoise

Cod Petals and Fork-smashed Zucchini

Cod Petals and Broccoli Buds

Rosemary Chickpea Purée

Free-Range Chicken Breast with Broccoli

Cream of Chicken

Button Mushroom Purée

Mousse of Avocado and Shrimp

Greek yogurt and herbs

Pop's Pasta:

Sliced Ham, Comté, au jus

Tomato and Goat Cheese

Pesto

Spinach-Mozzarella Tagliatelli Nests

8 months and up

20 to 25 mn

Potatoshow
French Style Mashed Potatoes

… at the market: 1 large Yukon Gold potato - 3 sprigs flat-leaf parsley
… at the grocery store: 2 Tbsp prepared baby formula - 1 small pat butter

and for a 1 year old: 1 more Yukon Gold potato - 1 Tbsp olive oil (instead of the prepared baby formula and butter) - 1 tiny pinch salt

vegetable peeler - paring knife - cutting board - fork

For 7 to 12 month olds: Rinse the potato, peel it with a vegetable peeler, wash it again, and dice it. Place the pieces in the steamer basket and cook for 15 minutes (water level 3).

Wash the parsley in water, dry it, and remove the leaves.

Throw the cooking juices away. Transfer the potato to the blending bowl and pulse once. Add the parsley leaves, milk, and butter. Pulse once more for a perfect homemade purée.

For babies 1 year and up: Prepare and cook the potatoes as above, and throw the cooking juices away. Prepare the parsley in the same way and crush the leaves with your hands. Next, smash the potatoes on a plate with a fork. Add the olive oil and parsley. Taste and lightly season, if necessary.

GOOD POINTS: *This recipe is simple but full of vitamins.*
The potato's richness places it far above other vegetables: carbohydrates, minerals, trace elements and let's not forget its vitamin content.
As for parsley, it contains calcium and vitamins (K, C, and carotene).
Olive oil is loaded with essential fatty acids.

7 months and up — 20 mn

Potatoshow

Potato Potage

… at the market: 1 large Yukon Gold or agria potato - 1 young leek

… at the grocery store: 1 pat of soft butter

For 1 year olds: A second potato - 1 tablespoon of olive oil - 1 pinch of salt

dish towel - vegetable peeler - paring knife - cutting board - bowl

For 7-12 month olds: Wash the leeks in running water and pat dry. Cut off the green parts. Finely cut 1 tbsp of the white. Wash the potato, peel, and wash again. Cut into long chunks. Cook cut leek and potato in the steamer for 15 min (water level 3). Keep the cooking juices in a bowl. Place the vegetables in the mixer and add a pad of soft butter. Pulse 1 to 2 times, adding a little bit of the cooking juices to obtain a homogenous purée.

For children over 1 year: Lightly season and drizzle with olive oil before serving.

GOOD POINTS: *A great combination! The soft fiber and diuretic properties of the leek work well with the potato's nutrients.*

7 months and up 25 mn

Potatoshaw
Crème vichyssoise

… at the market: 1 large Yukon Gold or agria potato - 1 small young leek - 3 or 4 sprigs of fresh parsley

… at the grocery store: 1 pat of soft butter

For a 1 year old: A second potato - 1 pinch of salt

dish towel - vegetable peeler - paring knife - bowl - plastic wrap - scissors

Prepare the potatoes and the white of the leek in the same way as for the Potato Potage (page 46). Cook in the steamer for 15 min (water level 3). Wash the parsley. Pat dry and cut finely using the scissors.

Keep the cooking juices. Transfer the vegetables into the mixer and add the parsley and the butter. Pulse 3 times, adding a little of the cooking juices between each pulse until the mixture becomes creamy. Pour into a bowl and cover with plastic wrap. Chill in the refrigerator and serve cold. Season lightly for older children.

GOOD POINTS: *Parsley's calcium and vitamins complement the potato's richness in carbohydrates, minerals, vitamins and trace elements.*

7 months and up · 20 mn

Cod Petals
and Fork-smashed Zucchini

… at the market: 1 small zucchini - 1 small Yukon Gold potato - 1 sprig of flat - leaf parsley - 1 small filet of cod 1.4 oz

… at the grocery store: a drizzle of olive oil

For children 1 year and up: 1 bay leaf - 3 or 4 leaves of thyme - 3 or 4 coriander seeds

cutting board - paring knife - scissors - 2 plates - plastic wrap - mixing bowl - fork

Cut the ends off the zucchini. Wash thoroughly under running water (we leave the skin on to give the dish color). Cut into quarters lengthwise. Remove the seeds with a knife and cut the quarters into small pieces.

Rinse the potato. Peel with the potato peeler and wash again. Cut into small pieces. Put the vegetables into the steamer and cook for 10 min (water level 2), and no more (to maintain the zucchini's green color). Throw away the cooking juices.

Cook the cod filet in the steamer for 3 min and no longer (water level 0.5), so it remains firm. Throw away the cooking juices.

While the cod is cooking, wash the parsley, shake dry, pick off the leaves and cut them into small pieces using the scissors. Place the raw parsley, and cooked potato and zucchini in a container. Smash with a fork. Use a mold to form the smashed vegetables into a circle and drizzle with olive oil.

Push on the cod filets with the fingertips to separate the petals. Place them on the circle of smashed zucchini.

GOOD POINTS: *Very good for the health. This recipe is light and easy to digest, which makes it excellent for your baby's first "real meals." Also, it doesn't take long to prepare. This dish unites two foods that are great for building a healthy body: a lean fish and great vegetables that can be eaten from 7 months.*

MORE WAYS TO LOVE IT: *For older babies (1 year), accentuate the Mediterranean flavor by fashioning a little cloth bag with 3 or 4 coriander seeds, thyme and 1 bay leaf (no more). Tie it up with a string and put it in the steamer before cooking the fish.*

7 months and up 15 mn

variation
Cod Petals and Broccoli Buds

… at the market: 1 small bunch fresh dill - 3 or 4 broccoli florets - 1/2 lemon - 1 small piece fresh cod (1.5 oz)

… at the grocery store: 1 pinch salt (for older children)

cutting board - small knife - 2 plates - plastic wrap - mixing bowl - scissors - fork

Shake the head of broccoli off in cool water. Cut off 3 or 4 florets. Place them in the steamer basket and cook for 5 minutes (water level 1).

Throw the cooking juices away. Smash the florets on a plate with a fork. Cover with plastic wrap to keep them warm.

Cut the dill up with scissors. Sprinkle (don't skimp!) it over the cooked cod (3 min, water level 0.5)

Layer the cod petals and the broccoli buds on baby's plate, just like a green and white mille-feuille. Finish by sprinkling with lemon juice.

MORE WAYS TO LOVE IT: *Ask the fishmonger to cut you a nice-looking cod filet that will stay firm during preparation and have him remove the bones.*

3 years and up — 5 mn the night before + 20 mn

Rosemary Chickpea Purée

… **at the market:** 1/4 green onion - 1 small sprig rosemary

… **at the grocery store:** 1/2 cup (2.75 oz) dry chickpeas - 1 Tbsp olive oil

2 bowls - strainer - cutting board - paring knife - whisk

The night before, soak the chickpeas in a large bowl of water to allow them to expand and soften during the night.

The following day, drain the chickpeas in a strainer and rinse them thoroughly under running water.

Remove the green onion's outer layer and thinly slice one quarter of it. Rinse the rosemary and pull its needle-like leaves off the stem.

Place the chickpeas, onion, and rosemary leaves in the steamer basket. Cook them for 15 minutes (water level 3). Pour the cooking juices into a bowl.

Transfer the contents of the steamer basket to the blending bowl. Pulse 2 or 3 times, adding a bit of cooking juice and a very small amount of olive oil between each pulse to obtain a homogenous consistency.

GOOD POINTS: *This dish lets us explore exotic flavors with all the virtues of chickpeas. They are nutritious, full of calories, and an excellent source of protein, carbohydrates, fiber, and folic acid (vitamin B9), a substance important in the development of a child's nervous system. However, the digestive system does not tolerate them until the age of 2 or 3.*

8 months and up · 30 mn

Free-range Chicken Breast with Broccoli

… at the market: 1 free-range chicken breast (about 3 oz) - 3 small broccoli florets - 3 small red potatoes - 1/2 small plum tomato - 1/2 white part of a thin pencil leek

… at the grocery store: 1 pinch salt - 1 thin drizzle olive oil - 1/4 turn of the pepper mill (white pepper) - a few grains fleur de sel

mixing bowl - saucepan, cutting board - paring knife - vegetable peeler - plate - plastic wrap

Remove the skin from the chicken breast, cut into small pieces, and place it directly into the steamer basket. Cook for 10 minutes (water level 2).

Prepare the vegetables: Cut 3 broccoli florets with a 1-inch stem. Remove the roots from the leek. Cut the top part of the leek into quarters lengthwise. Wash the vegetables under running water and shake them with the top facing down to get rid of any dirt. Cut the white part of the leek in half lengthwise and chop 1/2 of the white part into thin slices.

Remove the tomato stem. Cut the tomato in half (you will only use half). Rinse the potatoes in water, peel them with a vegetable peeler, and wash them before dicing them

When the diced chicken is cooked, throw the cooking juices away and transfer the meat to a plate. Cover it with plastic wrap to keep it warm.

Place the broccoli florets, the white part of the leek, half of the tomato, and the potato into the steamer basket. Cook them for 15 minutes (water level 3). Throw away the cooking juices. Transfer the vegetables to the blending bowl.

Pulse twice to obtain a purée, including the chicken for younger babies.

Spoon the vegetable purée into a soup bowl. For older babies, sprinkle the diced chicken over top. Drizzle with a small amount of olive oil.

For the biggest kids, lightly season and liven up the dish with a few grains of fleur de sel.

GOOD POINTS: *This is a healthy meal for delicate palates. The sweet taste of the red potato (full of calories) balances out the bitterness of the leek (soft fibers and diuretic action), as well as the acidity of the tomato (dripping with vitamins and minerals). And the broccoli adds a good dose of beta carotene (promotes growth and good vision) and especially vitamin C (boosts the body's immune system) to the mix.*

7 months and up — 20 mn

Cream of Chicken

… at the market: 1/2 carrot - 1 sweet potato (or turnip for children over 18 months) - 2 baby hearts of romaine lettuce - 1 oz of white farm-raised chicken

… at the grocery store: 2 Tbsp of prepared formula - 1 pat of butter

dish towel - vegetable peeler - cutting board - paring knife - saucepan

Take the butter out of the refrigerator.

Wash the vegetables under running water. Pat dry with a dish towel. Peel the carrot and cut it in half. Take one half and slice. Peel the sweet potato and cut it and the chicken into small pieces. Wash the carrot and the potatoes. Place the chicken and the cut vegetables in the steamer. Cook for 15 min (water level 3).

Pour the milk into the saucepan. Bring to a gentle boil.

Transfer the cooked vegetables into the mixer. Save the cooking juices in a bowl. Pulse 3 times, adding a little bit of the hot milk and butter between each pulse. If necessary, add some of the cooking juices to obtain a perfect velouté.

Pour the soup into the little gourmet's bowl, garnish with a "chiffonade" of shredded romaine lettuce.

GOOD POINTS: *To your baby's health! This dish is rich in protein (chicken) carbohydrates (potatoes), soft fiber (carrot and lettuce), and minerals and trace elements to spare!*

12 months and up 25 mn

Button Mushroom Purée

… at the market: 3.5 oz. Button mushrooms - 1 small Yukon Gold potato - 1/2 lemon

… at the grocery store: 2 Tbsp liquid crème fraiche - 1 tiny pinch of salt

mixing bowl - strainer - paring knife - cutting board - vegetable peeler

Prepare the Mushrooms: Trim the base. Clean the button mushrooms in lemon water. Rinse under running water and dry in a strainor.

Wash the potato, peel and dice it. Wash again.

Place the mushrooms and potato in the steamer basket with a splash of lemon juice and cook for 15 minutes (water level 3).

Throw the cooking juices away and transfer to the blender. Pulse 3 times, adding the cream little by little between each pulse to obtain a savory purée. Salt to taste.

GOOD POINTS: Raw, cooked, hot or cold, mushrooms work in all kinds of dishes. They are remarkably rich in minerals, trace elements and vitamins (B, D, and K). Babies often love them for how soft they feel in their mouths. They go well with meats, most notably with veal cakes (p. 130)!

2 years and up 10 mn

Mousse of Avocado and Shrimp

… at the market: 1/2 avocado - 1/2 lemon - 2 or 3 basil leaves - or fresh coriander
for toddlers (2-3 years old): 2 or 3 large pink Atlantic shrimp (cooked)

… at the grocery store: 1 thin drizzle olive oil

cutting board - paring knife - scissors

Wash the basil leaves (or fresh coriander) under running water. Cut them up with scissors.

Cut the lemon in half with a paring knife. To prevent the avocado from turning brown, do not wash off the knife, and rub the teaspoon with the lemon. Cut the avocado in half with the same knife, then use the spoon to remove half of the avocado flesh and place it in the blender.

Keep the avocado skin. Add 2 drops of lemon juice (and only 2 drops!), a thin drizzle of olive oil, and the herbs.

Blend : Pulse twice if you'd like to pique baby's curiosity by leaving a few avocado chunks in the mousse; or three times for a more homogenous, guacamole-style mousse. Stir with a spatula after each pulse.

For children over 2, you may add pink peeled shrimp that have been cut into small pieces (by hand or with 1 pulse in the blending bowl).

Spoon the mousse into a bowl or (even better) the avocado skin and decorate with a basil or coriander leaf.

GOOD POINTS: *Avocados introduce baby to a very refined taste; they are an important mixture of essential fatty acids (for the brain, nervous system, and retina) and vitamin E, which helps protect the fatty acids. But wait at least one year so that the digestive system can assimilate this rich fat.*

Shrimp are a wonderful source of protein and revitalizing mineral salts. But because of the risk of allergies, they must wait a little longer, till the age of 2 or 3.

MORE WAYS TO LOVE IT: *The fresh coriander refines the texture of the avocado. As the child grows, increase the quantity of lemon and decrease the number of pulses so as to chunks of avocado leave. Choose extremely fresh shrimp (with shiny, firm shells and a curved tail) or frozen ones.*

18 months and up · 15 mn

Greek yogurt and herbs

… at the market: 2 rounded Tbsp greek yogurt - 1 sprig chives - 1 sprig chervil - 1 sprig tarragon - 1/4 shallot

… at the grocery store: 1 thin drizzle walnut oil - stale bread for toasting (or crostinis)

dish towel - scissors - ramekin

Rinse the herbs under running water, shake them off, dry them in a dishtowel, and cut them into coarse pieces with scissors. Peel the shallot and chop it finely. Place 1 teaspoon of chives, 1 teaspoon of chervil, 1/2 teaspoon of tarragon, and 1/2 teaspoon of shallot into the blending bowl. Blend just a little (1 pulse) so as not to reduce it to a pulp. Add the greek yogurt, stir, and blend again (1 pulse). Pour the mixture into a ramekin. Toast the bread in a toaster or under the broiler. Serve it alongside the yogurt.

Right before serving, drizzle a bit of walnut oil over top. Let baby dip the bread right in.

MORE WAYS TO LOVE IT: *Start by having your baby taste the yogurt alone, then add a drizzle of oil, and then just one herb. Change the herb every time to figure out what your baby likes (or hates!).*

GOOD POINTS: *A daring recipe because it introduces baby to a whole new world of fine herbs and seasonings. But sensible because it brings together a bouquet of healthy ingredients and tastes that a baby of strong character will appreciate.*

8 months and up — 5 mn + time to cook pasta

Pop's Pasta
Sliced Ham, Comté, Au Jus

… at the market: 1 thick slice of cooked ham (1.5 oz) - 1 tsp au jus - 1 small piece of comté cheese (.75 oz)

… at the grocery store: 3 tsp of pasta (shells, alphabet, etc) - a drizzle of olive oil

paring knife - saucepan

Cut the excess fat off the ham and place in the blender. Pulse once. Remove the rind from the cheese and cut into small pieces.

Cook the pasta.

In a saucepan, mix the au jus and the ham over low heat. Once the ham has cooked and absorbed the au jus' color, add it to the pasta. Before serving, add the little pieces of cheese, which will melt slightly.

GOOD POINTS: *A great kid's version of the traditional ham served on Sundays.*

MORE WAYS TO LOVE IT: *Do you want your pasta to have a delicious au jus flavor as well? Cook them with 2 parts water and 1 part au jus.*

8 months and up 5 mn + time to cook pasta

Pop's Pasta
Tomato and Goat Cheese

… at the market: 1 oz of goat cheese - such as cabécou - 4 Tbsp of Tomato Fondue "Our Way" (see page 69) - 1 basil leaf

scissors - cutting board - paring knife

In this recipe, we will refine the Tomato Fondue to make a savory sauce.

Wash the basil under running water and cut it into small pieces with the scissors.

Cut the cheese into small pieces and put in the blender with the tomato fondue. Pulse 1 time. Add the basil and pulse 1 more time.

Serve over cooked pasta.

GOOD POINTS: *This recipe has a sweet and subtle flavor, and is nutritious and balanced from the combination of the cheese and tomato. Rich in vitamins (A, C, D) and minerals, as well as trace elements and calcium.*

MORE WAYS TO LOVE IT: *Tomato and goat's cheese? Try it with tortellini, for example!*

3 years and up — 5 mn + time to cook pasta

Pop's Pasta Pesto

MORE WAYS TO LOVE IT: *Add this pesto sauce to the Andalusian Gazpacho, chill in the refrigerator and serve cold.*

… at the market: 3 sprigs of basil - 0.35 oz parmesan reggiano - 1 Tbsp of pine nuts

… at the grocery store: 1 tiny pinch of salt - 4 Tbsp of olive oil

dish towel - paring knife - cheese grater

Wash the basil under running water, dry with a towel and remove the leaves by hand. Place them in the blending bowl. Use the knife to cut the rind off the parmesan and grate finely. Place in the mixer with the pine nuts. Add one tiny pinch of salt to keep the basil green. Pulse 3 times, adding the olive oil between each pulse to bind the ingredients to each other.

GOOD POINTS: *It's easy, delicious, fragrant and done in 5 minutes! Naturally, it goes well with pasta and brings some Italian flavor, and let's not forget all the virtues of the pine nut: rich in calories, it is as nutritious as the almond or the hazelnut but much easier on the digestive system.*

Pop's Pasta

Spinach-Mozzarella Tagliatelli Nests

… at the market: 3.5 oz. of fresh spinach - 3.5 oz of fresh tagliatelli nests - 1 Mozzarella di Bufala Campana

… at the grocery store: 1 drizzle of olive oil - 1 pinch of course salt

saucepan - strainer - paring knife - cutting board - bowl - salad bowl - fork

Boil a saucepan of water with the course salt and a drizzle of olive oil (to keep the pasta from sticking together).

Remove the stalk from the spinach and wash the leaves under running water. Place them in the steamer basket and cook for 5 min (water level 1). Throw the cooking juices away. Transfer the spinach into the blender. Pulse 1 time.

Place the tagliatelli in the boiling water and cook for 2 min (if they are fresh. Otherwise, cook for 8 min). Cut the mozzarella into little cubes.

Strain the pasta. Mix well with the spinach in a salad bowl. Add the mozzarella cubes.

Use a fork to turn the pasta and make 2 or 3 little nests and place them on a plate.

GOOD POINT:
Mozzarella is rich in protein.

MORE WAYS TO LOVE IT:
Set aside some tiny raw spinach leaves.
Use them to decorate the tagliatelli nests.

SUNNY DAYS

Meals for Summer and Springtime

Babaganoush

Tomato Fondue "Our Way"

Tomato Two Times

Melon Ball Soup

Mom and Baby, Two Peas in a Pod

Thyme for Green Bean Purée

Spring Velouté

Green Asparagus Velouté

Egg-Cellent Caponata

Quail's Egg à la Basquaise

Boiled Egg and Snow Peas

Andalusian Gazpacho

Zucchini Flan-tastic

Artichokes, leaf by leaf

Four Seasons of Purees and Casseroles

12 months and up — 25 mn

Babaganoush

… at the market: 1/2 small eggplant - 1/4 red pepper - 1/4 green pepper - 3 or 4 basil leaves

… at the grocery store: 1 tsp olive oil

scissors - bowl - cutting board - paring knife

Wash the basil leaves under running water and cut them into fine pieces with scissors. Set aside. Wash the 2 peppers, cut out their stems, remove the seeds, and cut them into quarters.

Dice 1/4 of the red pepper and 1/4 of the green pepper. Wash the eggplant, cut off its ends, peel it, and cut it in half. Cut half of the eggplant into pieces.

Place the diced pepper and eggplant pieces into the steamer basket and cook for 15 minutes (water level 3).

Throw the cooking juices away. Transfer the pepper and eggplant to the blending bowl. Pulse once.

Mix with the chopped basil leaves and olive oil before serving.

GOOD POINTS: *A Mediterranean taste. The smell of basil. The taste of olive oil (source of vitamin E and essential fatty acids). The sunny colors of the vegetables: the glossy deep purple eggplant, rich in fiber and potassium; and the shiny red and green pepper, rich in vitamins A and C.*

MORE WAYS TO LOVE IT: *Use the rest of the vegetables for the grown-ups: the leftover eggplant in ratatouille… and the extra peppers? For oil-cured peppers!*

6-8 months and up · 15 mn

Tomato Fondue "Our Way"

… at the market: 1 tomato - 2 basil leaves (4 leaves for children over 1 year old)

… at the grocery store: 1 drizzle olive oil - 1/2 tsp tomato paste (1 tsp for 1 year olds) - and a few ice cubes

for children over 1 year old: 1/4 green onion - 1/2 clove new garlic - 1 tiny pinch salt

small mixing bowl - small saucepan - cutting board - paring knife - slotted spoon - plastic wrap

Fill the mixing bowl with cold water and ice cubes. Boil water in the saucepan.

Clean the basil under running water, strip the leaves from the stem, and rip them into small pieces.

For little ones from 6 to 12 months: Cut out the tomato stem with a knife. Plunge the tomato in the boiling water for 20 seconds and then place it in the cold water. Dry it and peel the skin off. Cut the tomato in half, remove the seeds (easiest with the fingers) and place it in the steamer basket. Cook for 10 minutes (water level 2). Throw the cooking juices away. Transfer the tomato to the blending bowl. Add the tomato paste to brighten the color. Pulse once. Add the basil and pulse again. The resulting mixture will be slightly grainy. Pour into a bowl and drizzle with a bit of olive oil.

For babies over 1 year old: Remove the green onion's outer layer. Cut 1/4 of the green onion and 1/2 of the garlic clove into thin slices. Place them in the steamer basket with the tomato. Proceed as above. Use the basil to garnish the cooked fondue. Cool the dish, covered with plastic wrap, in the refrigerator for several minutes. Lightly salt it before serving.

Tomato Two Times

This recipe uses the Tomato Fondue recipe from page 69:

… at the market: 1 beefsteak tomato
… at the grocery store: a few grains of fleur de sel - 1/4 turn of white pepper from a pepper grinder

salad bowl - small saucepan - cutting board - dishtowel - serrated knife - plastic wrap

A version of the Tomato Fondue for special days.

First, prepare the fondue and set aside covered in plastic wrap. Use the knife to remove the stem. Cut out the tomato's fruity, juicy center. Remove the beafsteak tomato's skin by dipping it in boiling water for a few seconds, then transferring to a salad bowl full of cold water. The skin should peel off easily.

Cut the tomato into fine slices and place them on a plate. Cover with a thick layer of the warm tomato fondue. Season with a very small amount of fleur de sel and white pepper.

GOOD POINTS: *The tomato, queen of summer foods, is light, thirst-quenching and rich in vitamins (especially C), minerals and trace elements. When ripe, cooked and with the skin and seeds (irritants) removed, it can be eaten from 6 months, first in potages and then in fondue. Children over 1 year can eat it raw and firm, but still without the skin.*

MORE WAYS TO LOVE IT: *You can use the beefsteak potato as a container for the fondue: peel it, cut the top off and dig out the center with a spoon. Fill the cavity with the warm tomato fondue.*

8 months and up — 5 mn

Melon Ball Soup

… at the market: 1 small fresh ripe melon (cantaloupe or Crenshaw) - 2 fresh mint leaves

scissors - small knife - teaspoon - melon baller - bowl

Wash the melon under running water and cut it in half. Remove the seeds with a spoon.

Rinse the mint leaves under running water and cut them up with scissors.

Take one half of the melon and cut it into two quarters. You will only use one of these quarters.

Peel it with the knife and poke the flesh several times with a fork. Cut the flesh into small pieces. Place them in the blending bowl. Pulse twice, adding a small amount (about 1 tablespoon) of slightly mineralized water between the pulses to obtain a light soup.

Use the melon baller to scoop little balls from the second half of the melon. Place the melon balls in a bowl and set aside.

Pour the melon soup into half of the rind, add the melon balls, and sprinkle with mint.

GOOD POINTS: *This soup refreshes in summer and its slightly sweet taste makes it a great thirst-quencher. Babies love it from the bottle. Mint aids digestion (and helps with headaches, too) and contains a good amount of vitamins (A and B). Melon is great for preventing fatigue. Teeming with vitamins (especially vitamin C), it rivals the kiwi.*

MORE WAYS TO LOVE IT: *Without the mint, you can give this melon soup to baby through a bottle when he or she needs something to drink. For older babies, add strawberries (make sure they are not allergic) to the melon balls. Serve in the melon shell on a plate over a bed of ice cubes.*

10 months and up · 20 mn

Mom and Baby, Two Peas in a Pod

… at the market: 10 garden peapods - 1 teaspoon of follow-up formula

for a 1 year old: 15 garden peapods - 1/2 green onion

… at the grocery store: 1 small pat salted butter - 1 or 2 croutons

cutting board - paring knife - bowl - Chinois

For little ones from 10 to 12 months: Wash the pods. Shell half of the peas and leave the rest. Place all of the shelled and unshelled peas in the steamer basket. Cook for 15 minutes (water level 3). Pour the cooking juices into a bowl. Transfer the cooked peas to the blending bowl. Blend to obtain a smooth consistency (2 pulses), adding the milk between the first and second pulse.

For babies 1 year and up: Prepare the peas as above. Set aside 3 or 4 raw peas for decoration. Place the peas in the steamer basket. Peel the onion, cut it in half, and slice half of it thinly. Add it to the steamer basket. Cook for 15 min (water level 3).

Pour the cooking juices into a bowl, and transfer the onions to the blending bowl. Pulse twice to obtain a smooth consistency, adding some of the cooking juices between the first and second pulse for a creamy purée. If you would like to turn this purée into a delicious velouté, pulse a third time and add more of the cooking juices to obtain a liquid, homogenous consistency. Strain the mixture through the Chinois to obtain a perfectly thin velouté and place in the refrigerator for 10 minutes so that it keeps its pretty green color…

To garnish the purée for older children, make a little crouton by toasting stale bread. Spread a little salted butter on it. Take the peas you've saved and cut them into quarters (yes, really!). Place the quarters on top of the crouton and float the little "boat" on top of the purée.

GOOD POINTS: *Peas are so sweet and tender that baby will like them right away, which makes moms happy because they are rich in carbohydrates (calories), protein (for building a strong body), and fiber (intestinal transit). Fresh (and organic!) or frozen, peas can be given to baby in purées starting at 10 months. But no whole peas before age 3, so that they don't take a trip down the "wrong tube!"*

MORE WAYS TO LOVE IT: *For connoisseurs, serve this purée with a scrambled egg topped with a chopped coriander leaf (to be added at the last moment)…*

MORE WAYS TO LOVE IT: *For the "grown-up menu," green bean purée goes best with ham, poultry, and fish. Serve it alone or with another purée to add color and flavor.*

Thyme for Green Bean Purée

… at the market: 1/3 cup (1.5 oz) thin French-style green beans - 1/2 baking potato - 1 small sprig wild thyme

for a 1-year old: 2/3 cup (3 oz) thin French-style green beans - 1/4 green onion - 1/2 baking potato - 1 sprig wild thyme

… at the grocery store: 1 thin drizzle olive oil

cutting board - vegetable peeler - paring knife - dish cloth bowl

For little ones from 6 to 12 months: Wash the green beans and snap off their ends. Rinse the potato under running water, peel it with the vegetable peeler, and wash it again before cutting half of it into pieces. Wash the wild thyme and pat it dry. Place it in the steamer basket with the chopped potato and cook for 10 minutes (water level 2). Collect the cooking juices in a bowl. Transfer the steamer basket contents to the blending bowl. Pulse twice, adding a small amount of cooking juices between the pulses in order to obtain the desired consistency.

For babies 1 year and up: Before cooking, remove the green onion's outer layer and thinly slice the white part. Cook 1/4 of it and for 10 minutes. Throw away the cooking juices, and add the onion to the other vegetables. Before blending, drizzle a small amount of olive oil into the blending bowl. This intensifies the taste of the green beans while complimenting the flavor of the wild thyme.

GOOD POINTS: *Green beans provide baby with a generous amount of minerals (potassium, magnesium, calcium, sulfur, iron, etc.), vitamins (C, A, and B9 or folic acid, among others), and soft fiber. All that and they are easy on the digestive system, even at an early age.*

15 months and up — 25 mn

Spring Velouté

… at the market: 1.75 oz shelled fresh peas - 1/2 green onion - 1.75 oz spring carrots - 1.75 oz French-style green beans - 1.75 oz fava beans
… at the grocery store: 1 small pat of butter - 1 tiny pinch of salt

paring knife - cutting board - vegetable peeler

Wash the vegetables under running water. Peel the onion and finely chop one half. Shell the peas and fava beans and remove the membranes (see fava bean velouté on page 106). Break the ends off the green beans. Peel the carrot with the vegetable peeler and cut into thin slices.

Place the onion peas, fava beans, green beans, and carrots in the steamer basket. Cook for 15 minutes (water level 3).

Throw away the cooking juices and place the vegetables in the blender.

Pulse 3 times, adding a little bit of slightly mineralized water between each pulse to obtain a thin velouté. Taste and season with a little salt (and, when your child is older, a little bit of white pepper).

Serve in a dish with a melting pat of butter in the center.

GOOD POINTS: *The humble fava bean hides a wealth of nutrition: rich in carbohydrates, protides, fiber, vitamins (especially B and C, and even when dried). The fava beans' virtues partner well with the peas' proteins (the most of any green vegetable), the minerals and soft fibers of the green beans and the carrots sweet flavor. There are a lot of good things in this recipe, and a lot of flavor! To be served again and again…*

12 months and up · 20 mn

Green Asparagus Velouté

… at the market: 1 dozen thin green asparagus spears - 1/2 green onion - 3 spinach leaves

… at the grocery store: 1 tiny pinch salt - 1 thin drizzle olive oil - and a few ice cubes

cutting board - paring knife - mandoline - chinois - bowl

Stem the spinach leaves. Thoroughly wash the leaves in several rounds of cool water. Set aside.

Remove the green onion's outer layer. Cut the onion in half and thinly slice the half to be used. Set aside.

Gently wash the asparagus one by one. Cut off the hard, dirty end (1 inch) and throw them away. Remove their small "leaves" with a paring knife. Cut the asparagus into thin slices. Place them, along with the 1/2 green onion, into the steamer basket and cook for 15 minutes (water level 3). Pour the cooking juices into a bowl.

Place the cooked asparagus and onions, plus the raw spinach leaves, in the blending bowl.

Blend, adding a small amount of cooking juices between each pulse, depending on the desired consistency. Pulse once for a purée with a few asparagus chunks; twice for a more homogenous consistency; or three times for a velouté that will be perfect if you strain it through a Chinois. Salt to taste (if necessary). Pour into a bowl and decorate with a thin drizzle of olive oil.

GOOD POINTS: *This is a sweet, simple, and delicately flavored velouté. The spinach brings out the color and taste in this dish.*

It's a fresh-tasting recipe to be eaten cold in the summer. It is jam-packed with vitamins and minerals, especially B vitamins and potassium. This little gem has a good amount of soft fibers, which aids intestinal transit, and is a well-known diuretic.

MORE WAYS TO LOVE IT: *Set aside 2 raw asparagus tips, and thinly slice with a mandoline. Garnish the velouté with the sliced asparagus before serving. This allows baby to discover how asparagus tastes both raw and cooked, hot and cold.*

3 years and up · 25 mn

Egg-cellent Caponata

… at the market: 1/2 eggplant - 1 small plum tomato - 1 green onion - 1/2 sweet pepper - 1 clove new garlic - a few basil leaves and sprigs flat-leaf parsley - 3 large pinches pine nuts - 1 “farm-fresh” free-range egg - 1 slice lean boiled ham - sliced thinly like prosciutto

… at the grocery store: 1 thin drizzle olive oil - 1 tiny pinch salt

cutting board - paring knife - vegetable peeler - scissors - saucepan - slotted spoon

Wash the vegetables under running water.

Cut the stem out of the pepper, cut the pepper into quarters, and remove the white membranes and seeds. Dice the 2 quarters to be used. Peel and quarter the tomato, and then dice the pieces.

Peel the eggplant with a vegetable peeler, cut it in half, and cut the half you are going to use into 3 or 4 slices. Remove the green onion’s outer layer. Thinly slice the green onion and garlic clove, but use just a little of each to season the caponata.

Place the vegetables in the steamer basket and cook for 15 minutes (water level 3).

Wash the herbs under running water and cut them up finely using scissors (except for one basil leaf, which you should keep for garnish). Cut the excess fat off the ham and place it on a dish.

To cook the poached egg, boil salted water in a saucepan. Break the egg into the saucepan, wait 5 minutes, and remove it with a slotted spoon. Place the egg on top of the thinly sliced ham. Fold the ham around the egg like a little present.

When the vegetables are cooked, throw the cooking juices away and transfer to the blending bowl along with the herbs, pine nuts,

and olive oil. Pulse once to obtain a caviar-like consistency with a few chunks, or twice for a frothy consistency. Salt to taste.

Spoon the caponata onto the plate next to the ham-egg "present," and decorate it with the basil leaf to add a bit of color.

GOOD POINTS: *This dish has a very subtle taste and is a complete, balanced meal: fiber and potassium in the eggplant; calcium and vitamin K in the parsley; vitamins A and C found in sweet peppers; proteins in pine nuts, an excellent brain food; proteins and vitamin B1 in boiled ham.*

Plus the egg, an almost perfect food.

MORE WAYS TO LOVE IT: *This recipe is also delicious served cold on summer days.*

2 years and up · 20 mn

Quail's Egg à la Basquaise

… at the market: 1/2 tomato - 1/2 oz. red pepper - 1/2 oz. green pepper - 1/2 oz. yellow pepper - 1/4 clove of pink garlic - 1/2 green onion - 2 quail's eggs or 1 or 2 small chicken eggs

… at the grocery store: 1 tsp of tomato paste - 1 small pat of butter - 1 pinch of salt - 1/4 turn of white pepper from a pepper grinder

paring knife - cutting board - small non-stick frying pan

Cut the ends off the peppers and the stems off the tomatoes. Wash under running water and cut into quarters. Remove the seeds from the peppers and finely cut .5 oz. of each pepper (about 1 Tbsp) as well as 1/2 the tomato. Remove the onion's outer skin and finely cut 1/2. Place the onions, peppers and tomatoes in the steamer with the 1/4 clove of garlic and the tomato paste on top. Cook for 15 min (water level 3) and throw away the cooking juices. Transfer to the blender. Add olive oil and pulse 3 times. Shape the minced vegetables into 2 domes on a plate. Use a knife to cut the top of the shell off the quail's egg, as you would for a hard boiled egg. Heat the butter in a frying pan until it sizzles, lightly season and use to cook the eggs sunny-side up. Serve on top of the domes.

GOOD POINTS: *A quail's egg, yes! It has the same flavors as a chicken's egg but is more subtle and one third the size. With its brown spotted shell, it contains vitamins A, B, D, E and K and it is an important source of amino acids, which are essential for growth.*

MORE WAYS TO LOVE IT: *You can also use the quail's eggs to make shirred eggs. In a buttered ramekin, break 2 quail's eggs and add 0.7 oz of diced boiled ham. Cook for 3 min in a double boiler (or in a steamer) before drizzling a little bit of liquid cream on top.*

2 years and up — 15 mn

Boiled Egg and Snow Peas

… at the market: 3-3 1/2 oz. snow peas - one small piece of fresh parmesan cheese (a little less than 1 oz) - 1 extra fresh free-range chicken egg
… at the grocery store: 1 light drizzle of olive oil - a few drops of vinegar

cutting board - paring knife - potato peeler - small saucepan

Wash the snow peas and place in the steamer. Cook for 10 minutes (water level 2). While they cook, use the potato peeler to peel a few slices of parmesan and set them aside.

Boil some water with a little vinegar (do not add salt). Place the whole egg in a teaspoon and lower into the boiling water.
Be careful not to let the egg hit the bottom of the pan too hard and break. Allow to cook for exactly 3 1/2 min. Present in an egg cup on the baby's plate.

When the snow peas are finished cooking, cut them in half lengthwise (careful not to burn yourself!). Place them next to the egg and garnish with the cheese slices and a light drizzling of olive oil. The snow peas are used for dipping in the yolk.

__GOOD POINTS:__ A fun way to introduce the child's tastes to a vegetable as old as time. Snow peas are rich in vitamins A, B and C, as well as minerals and fiber.

The egg is a point of reference for healthy eating. Within its shell you will find all the nutrients necessary for a good meal. Buy eggs that are marked as "fresh" and have the packaging date clearly displayed. They should be less than a week old. Never store eggs next to strong smelling foods. Their permeable shells will absorb the taste.

__MORE WAYS TO LOVE IT:__ Babies like fresh parmesan because it has flavor but it is not too strong.

12 months and up

20 mn

Andalusian Gazpacho

… at the market: 1/4 small cucumber - 1 large tomato - 1/4 white onion - 0.35 oz red pepper - 3 sprigs basil - 1 celery stalk - 1 clove new garlic

… at the grocery store: 1 Tsp tomato paste - 1 drizzle Sherry vinegar - 1 tbsp crushed ice

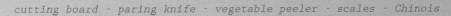

cutting board - paring knife - vegetable peeler - scales - Chinois

Remove the leaves from the sprigs of basil. Rinse the basil leaves, cucumber, tomato, celery, and pepper under running water. Peel the cucumber and cut it into quarters. Remove the tomato's stem and the stringy fibers from the celery stalk (from the bottom to the top).

Remove the seeds from the pepper and cut a slice of about 0.35 oz. Cut the basil leaves, 1/4 cucumber, tomato, celery stalk, and pepper slice into pieces. Peel the onion. Cut 1/4 of it and the garlic clove into small pieces.

Place the vegetables into the blending bowl. Add the tomato paste and crushed ice. Blend well (3 pulses) to obtain an even consistency If a few chunks still remain after blending, strain the gazpacho through a Chinois.

Add a drizzle of Sherry vinegar to take away any acidity and lightly enhance the gazpacho's aromas. Serve cool with a tiny dribble of pesto on special days.

GOOD POINTS: *This recipe is not only fresh, thirst-quenching, light,and flavorfuly but also extremely nutritional. Cucumbers, tomatoes, and peppers are all good sources of minerals, trace elements, and vitamins (especially C and A).*

GOOD POINTS: *A light and complete meal, easily digestible and refreshing, this flan melts on the tongue and is sweet to the palate. The calcium found in fromage blanc teams up perfectly with the phosphorus found in eggs and makes for healthy bones and beautiful teeth. The density of minerals and the mix of vitamins found in zucchini will get baby into shape.*

12 months and up — 30 mn

Zucchini Flan-tastic

… at the market: 1 zucchini (around 5.25 oz) - 1 “farm-fresh” free-range egg - 2 Tbsp fat-free fromage blanc - 1 small pat butter + butter for the ramekin

cutting board - pastry brush - paring knife - whisk - small mixing bowl - ramekin - small gratin dish

Preheat the oven to 300 °F (gas 3).

Butter the ramekin (from the bottom to the top with a pastry brush, so that the flan rises easily), and place it in the refrigerator to cool.

Wash the zucchini thoroughly under running water because you will leave the skin on to add a little color to the dish. Cut into quarters lengthwise. If it contains too many seeds, remove them with a spoon. Place the pieces in the steamer basket and cook for 5 minutes (water level 1).

Throw the cooking juices away. Transfer the zucchini to the blending bowl. Blend to obtain a homogenous consistency (2 or 3 pulses). Let cool.

Beat the egg in a mixing bowl. Add the fromage blanc, a small pat of butter, and the cooled zucchini. Mix vigorously. Fill the ramekin half full with this mixture.

Reduce the oven temperature to 250 °F (gas 2). Pour a little bit of water in the gratin dish. Place the ramekin in it. Place this double boiler in the oven for 15 to 20 minutes.

Check that the flan is done by inserting a knife in the center. If the blade comes out clean, the flan is ready for the tasting.

18 months and up · 25 mn

Artichokes, Leaf by Leaf

… at the market: 2 artichokes - 1/4 lemon
… at the grocery store: .5 oz (about 2 tablespoons) flour - a drizzle of walnut oil

saucepan - knife - teaspoon

On special days, dress up the artichoke purée recipe (My First Artichoke, p. 31) with a presentation that everybody is sure to love. Cook a second whole artichoke (washed, with the stem broken by hand) in a white court-bouillon. Heat water in a pot with 2 tablespoons of flour and the juice of one quarter of a lemon. When the water begins to boil, place the artichoke in the pot and let it cook uncovered for 20 minutes.

While it is cooking, prepare artichoke purée with the Babycook (page 31).

Once the second artichoke is finished cooking in the court bouillon, remove all of the leaves and then the choke with a teaspoon.

Arrange a dozen or so of the tender leaves around the artichoke heart like a flower and fill with the artichoke purée. Drizzle with a small amount of walnut oil.

GOOD POINTS: *The artichoke in all its forms: the savory heart, the tender leaves and the little chunks in the purée. Its taste goes wonderfully with the bittersweet flavor of the walnuts. They're good for the heart, arteries and the baby's brain development (omega-3).*

Careful: first make sure that baby is not allergic to nuts!

Four Seasons of Purées and Casseroles

18 months and up — 25 mn

GOOD POINTS: *A handful of small new vegetables, tender and fresh. Serve these flavorful veggies to smaller babies as a purée, and in colorful little pieces in a mini casserole dish to older babies, and know that your baby, whatever his or her age, is getting a great mix of minerals and vitamins.*

Purée of Spring Vegetables

… at the market: 4 fresh peapods - 1 small new carrot - 1 new turnip - 1 green onion - 1 small new fennel bulb - 1 small purple artichoke - 10 market-fresh fava bean pods - 2 round baby potatoes - 4 sprigs flat-leaf parsley

… at the grocery store: 1 thin drizzle olive oil - 1 pat butter - a few grains of fleur de sel - 1/4 turn of the pepper mill (white pepper)

cutting board - vegetable peeler - scissors - paring knife -bowl

MORE WAYS TO LOVE IT:
Leave the skin on the baby potatoes because they add a nice taste and are a good source of vitamins.

Rinse the vegetables in water and then peel each of them, including the onions. Wash them thoroughly. Leave them whole if they are small. Otherwise, cut them into 2 or 3 pieces.

Shell the peas. Shell the fava beans as well, and remove their skin by pinching each bean so it slips out of the skin. Cut the fava beans in 2.

Prepare the artichoke last. Cut the stem about 1 inch from the leaves. Peel the remaining stem with a knife. Use your hands to remove the leaves from the base of the artichoke. Then cut off the tops of the leaves 1/3 of the way from the top. Place all of the vegetables (except for the parsley) into the steamer basket and cook them for a good 15 minutes (water level 3).

Wash the parsley, cut it up with scissors, and set aside.

Once everything is cooked, pour the cooking juices into a bowl. Transfer all of the vegetables to the blending bowl. Pulse at least 3 times for an even purée, adding a small amount of the cooking juices between each pulse.

Spoon the spring purée onto a plate. Drizzle a small amount of olive oil over it, and sprinkle it with a few grains of fleur de sel and chopped parsley.

Purée of Summer Vegetables

… at the market: 1 zucchini with blossom - 2 round red radishes - 2 small thin asparagus spears - 10 extra-thin green beans

The yellow zucchini flower is a simple touch that you can add at the end to make the dish pretty. Remove it from the zucchini and shape it with a knife, for example, into the form of a dragon's crest.

Wash the vegetables under running water, peel and dice them.

Snap off the ends of the green beans. Cut of the dirty ends of the asparagus spears and remove their little "leaves."
Remove the ends of the zucchini and cut it in half lengthwise.

Add these to the vegetables from the Purée of Spring Vegetables (see p. 92). Cook and blend in the same way, and spoon onto a plate. But finish off the dish with the zucchini flower!

GOOD POINTS: *Even better than the spring purée! The summer adds its seasonal vegetables, ripened in the warm sun.*

MORE WAYS TO LOVE IT: *Reduce the cooking juices in a saucepan and add a pat of butter. Use a pastry brush to coat the vegetables with the reduction and serve them sparkling in a glass casserole dish. It's the "Summer Casserole!"*

Purée of Winter Vegetables

Add the following ingredients to the fall purée:

… at the market: 1 salsify root - 5 or 6 (concord) grapes

Proceed as on page 95: wash, peel and cut the fruits and vegetables for the autumn purée.

Carefully rinse the salsify root under running water to wash out the dirt. Peel it with a vegetable peeler and cut it into pieces that are 1½ to 2 inches long. Place it in lemon water (along with the Swiss chard) so that it does not brown before cooking with the rest of the fruits and vegetables.

Serve with a drizzle of olive oil, a pat of butter and a very small amount of salt and pepper. Place the (pre-washed) grapes on top.

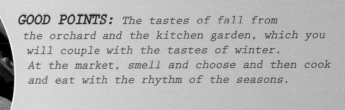

GOOD POINTS: *The tastes of fall from the orchard and the kitchen garden, which you will couple with the tastes of winter. At the market, smell and choose and then cook and eat with the rhythm of the seasons.*

Puree of Fall Vegetables

… at the market: 1 small pumpkin slice (1/4 cup once the rind is removed) - 1 leaf Swiss chard - 1 small chestnut (frozen!) - 1/2 Bosc pear - 1/2 Jonathan apple - 1 red potato - 1 green onion - 1/2 lemon

… at the grocery store: 1 thin drizzle olive oil - 1 pat butter - a few grains of fleur de sel - 1/4 turn of the pepper mill (white pepper)

mixing bowl - cutting board - paring knife - vegetable peeler - bowl

Fill a mixing bowl with lemon water. Wash the Swiss chard and cut the white part away from the green (keep it for another meal). Peel the white part with a vegetable peeler so as to remove all the stringy fibers. Place it in the lemon water in the mixing bowl.

Wash the potato and peel it with a vegetable peeler. Remove the pumpkin rind, seeds, and stringy flesh. Remove the green onion's outer layer. Wash the apple and pear, peel them, cut them in half, and remove their cores. Wash the chestnut, score its shell so that it comes off more easily, and cut it in half.
Cut the fruits and vegetables into pieces (everything must fit in the steamer basket!). Cook them all for a good 15 minutes (water level 3).

Pour the cooking juices into a bowl. Transfer the contents of the steamer basket to the blending bowl. Pulse twice, adding 2 tablespoons of cooking juices between pulses, to obtain a thin purée. Or pulse only once, and add 1 tablespoon of cooking juices, to obtain a thicker purée.

Spoon onto a plate. Add a pat of butter and a drizzle of olive oil. Mix, taste, and season with some fleur de sel and a tiny bit of white pepper if necessary.

BABY COLD DAY
Meals for Fall and Winter

Lentil and Dry-Cured Ham Velouté

Mom's little Ham

White bean Soup

Cauliflower Curry in a Hurry

Fava Bean Velouté

Cream of Spinach

Let's Dive into Endives

Mini Filet of Beef and Pan-Fried Potatoes

Exotic Tastes:

Pytt-i-Panna

Swedish Meatballs

My First Couscous

Mary Had a Little Lamb (Kefta)

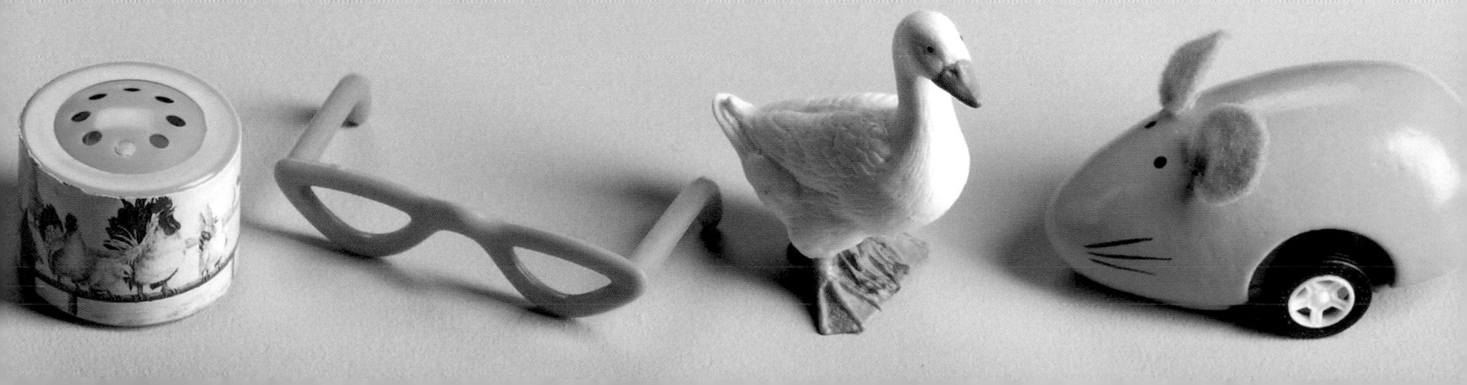

MORE WAYS TO LOVE IT: *To change the flavor a little, remove the cured ham from the cooking process and cut in into fine pieces that can be wrapped around grissini and dipped in the velouté!*

Make homemade croutons and go even crunchier! Take a slice of sandwich bread, remove the crust with a knife, and cut the center into small cubes. Toast them with a drizzle of grapeseed oil in a frying pan until golden brown (not dark brown though!). Soak up some of the oil by letting them cool on a paper towel.

GOOD POINTS: *Lentils have the second highest amount of protein of all legumes, right behind soybeans, and are richer in carbohydrates than whole grains. They also contain seven times more iron than spinach.*

18 months and up · 20 mn

Lentil and Dry-Cured Ham Velouté

… at the market: 1/3 cup green lentils - 1/2 celery stalk - 1/2 carrot - 1 sprig thyme - 1 slice dry-cured ham (0.35 oz)

… at the grocery store: 1 slice sandwich bread - 1 drizzle grapeseed oil - 1 Tbsp thick crème fraîche - 1 tiny pinch salt

mixing bowl - strainer - saucepan - cutting board - paring knife - vegetable peeler - parchment paper - nonstick pan - paper towel - bowl

Prepare the lentils the night before. Wash them thoroughly by picking them over on the palm of your hand to eliminate any possible stones. Leave them to soak overnight in a mixing bowl full of water so that they expand and become softer.

The following day, drain the lentils using a strainer. Blanch them on the stove by placing them in boiling water for 30 seconds. Drain them again.

Cut the celery stalk in half lengthwise. Wash the half that you are going to use and cut it into small pieces. Wash half of the carrot, peel it, and cut it into pieces. Rinse the thyme under running water. Dice the ham.

Line the bottom of the steamer basket with 2 layers of parchment paper. Pour in the lentils. Add the carrot, celery, thyme, and dry-cured ham. Cook everything for 15 minutes (water level 3). Pour the cooking juices into a separate bowl. Transfer the vegetables to the blending bowl. Pulse three times, adding some cooking juices between each pulse to obtain a nice-looking velouté. Don't skimp on the cooking juices, because this velouté tends to be rather thick.

Pour the velouté into a soup bowl. Spoon a dollop of crème fraîche onto the middle. Sprinkle the croutons around it if you choose to do so (see left). Serve right away, while the crème is still melting.

18 months and up · 20 mn

MORE WAYS TO LOVE IT: *The sage brings out the flavor of ham, rabbit and veal. I substitute smoked prosciutto for the bone-in ham for a more pronounced flavor.*

Mom's Little Ham

… at the market: 1/4 celery root (2.75 oz) - 1 large Yukon Gold potato - 1/2 carrot - 1 small handful thin French-style green beans - 1 small sage leaf - 1 slice (1.5 oz) bone-in ham

… at the grocery store: 1 Tbsp prepared milk-based pediatric nutritional supplement - 1 thin drizzle olive oil - 1 tiny pinch salt

cutting board - paring knife - vegetable peeler

Rinse all of the vegetables under running water. Snap off the ends of the green beans. Peel the potato, carrot, and celery root with the vegetable peeler. Use only half of the carrot and a quarter of the celery. Cut the vegetables into equal-sized pieces, rinse them, and place them in the steamer.

Cook for 15 min (water level 3).

Remove the fat from the ham and cut it into small pieces.

Throw the cooking juices away. Transfer the cooked vegetables to the blending bowl. Add the milk and the sage leaf. Pulse 3 times to obtain a purée.

Spoon the purée onto a plate, add a tiny bit of salt (for older babies), and drizzle a bit of olive oil on top. Sprinkle the bits of ham over the purée.

18 months and up 5 mn the day before + 20 mn

White Bean Soup

… at the market: 3.5 oz. of dried white beans - 1/2 carrot - 1/4 onion - 1/2 clove of garlic
… at the grocery store: 1 Tbsp olive oil

large mixing bowl - bowl - strainer - vegetable peeler - paring knife

Prepare the beans the day before. Place in a salad bowl filled with water and cover with plastic wrap. Place in the refrigerator. Allow to soak overnight so that they expand and become softer.

The day of cooking, remove them from the refrigerator and drain.

Wash the carrot. Peel with the vegetable peeler and cut into quarters. Cut into small cubes and wash. Peel the outer skin off the onion and finely cut 1/4 of the onion. Peel the garlic and cut off the germ with a knife. Cut in two pieces and use only half.

Place the carrot, onion and garlic in the steamer and cook for 15 min (water level 3). Save the cooking juices in a bowl.

Transfer the vegetables into the blender. Add olive oil and pulse 3 times, being careful to add just enough of the juices to obtain a fluid soup with no lumps.

GOOD POINTS: *Beans are nourishing, and rich in proteins, vitamins and mineral salts. Dried beans are a great source of potassium and folic acid, as well as of magnesium and iron. They also contain copper, zinc, phosphorus, thiamine, niacin and vitamin B6.*

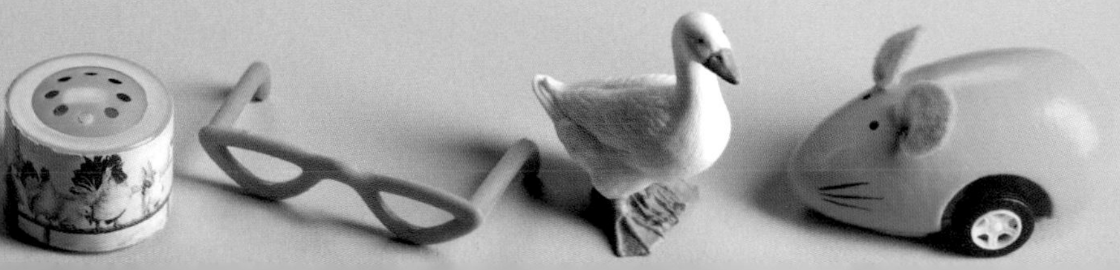

Cauliflower Curry in a Hurry

… at the market: 1 cauliflower

… at the grocery store: 3 or 4 Tbsp prepared milk-based pediatric nutritional supplement (or prepared baby formula for the youngest babies) - 1/4 tsp curry (optional) - a few drops white vinegar

large bowl - paring knife - 2 small saucepans - slotted spoon - bowl

Wash the cauliflower in running water. Let it soak for a few minutes in the vinegar water. Cut the biggest florets in half, leaving only 1-inch stems. Place 3 or 4 florets in the steamer basket and cook them for 15 minutes (water level 3).

Boil water in a saucepan. Drop 3 or 4 very small cauliflower florets in the boiling water and leave them to cook “English style” for 30 seconds. Remove them with a slotted spoon.

In a second saucepan, heat 3 or 4 tablespoons of milk supplement or formula (the amount depends on the desired consistency of the dish).

When the vegetables have been steamed, collect the cooking juices in a bowl and add two tsp to the heated milk.

Transfer the cooked cauliflower to the blending bowl.
Add 1/4 teaspoon of curry if desired. Pulse once. Add the heated milk from the second saucepan and pulse once more.

Pour the cream-colored velouté into a soup bowl. Place the little blanched florets on top.

MORE WAYS TO LOVE IT: *If you add less cooking juices and prepared milk-based pediatric nutritional supplement, you will obtain a cauliflower purée whose consistency you can adapt to your baby's preferences.*

GOOD POINTS: *It's fun to discover cauliflower cooked and (almost) raw. This vegetable deserves to be loved for its concentration in vitamin C and its protective micronutrients, plus its density in soft fiber but especially for its gentle, delicate flavor.*

15 months and up 15 mn

GOOD POINTS: *Fava beans are a good source of calories because they are rich in carbohydrates, fiber, and protein. They are tender and easy to digest when cooked.*

Fava Bean Velouté

… at the market: 2/3 cups (3.5 oz) fava beans - 1/2 baking potato - 1/4 green onion - 1/2 clove new garlic - 1 sprig savory (if necessary)

… at the grocery store: 1 Tbsp olive oil

cutting board - paring knife - vegetable peeler - bowl - Chinois if necessary

Shell the fava beans and remove their skin by pinching each bean so it slips out. Cut them in half. Rinse the potato under running water, peel it with the vegetable peeler, and wash it again. Dice the half that you are going to use. Remove the green onion's outer layer. Thinly slice one quarter of it. Cut the garlic clove in half. Place the vegetables, and the garlic into the steamer basket. If you prefer to make purée, add the savory.
Cook for 10 minutes (water level 2).

Pour the cooking juices into a bowl. Transfer the steamer basket's contents to the blending bowl.

Pulse twice for a purée and three times for a velouté, adding enough of the cooking juices between each pulse to obtain the desired consistency.

MORE WAYS TO LOVE IT:
When your children are younger, replace the cooking juices in this recipe with prepared milk-based pediatric nutritional supplement, making the velouté sweeter and the fava bean easier for babies to enjoy.

8 months and up 10 mn

MORE WAYS TO LOVE IT: *After 2-3 years, instead of water use 7 Tbsp of crème fraiche and add a tiny bit of garlic, shallots and a few small pieces of tomato (seeded and skinned) for a "Florentine" variation.*

Cream of Spinach

… at the market: 7 cups (7 oz) fresh spinach

… at the grocery store: 1 Tbsp heavy cream

for older children: 1 tiny pinch salt - 1/4 turn of pepper from a pepper mill

dish towel - spatula

Stem the spinach leaves and wash them in a colander under running water. Wipe them with a towel then place them in the steamer basket and cook for 5 minutes (water level 1).

Throw the cooking juices away. Transfer the spinach to the blending bowl. Add a little slightly mineralized water and pulse once. Add the cream and pulse a second time, stirring with the spatula between pulses.

The resulting mixture will be a creamy purée. Add a little salt for older children.

GOOD POINTS: *The king of fiber! Spinach gently stimulates intestinal transit. With its trifecta of potassium, calcium and magnesium and its antioxydants and pigments (carotene, chlorophyll), which help the body assimilate vitamin C (this works even better when paired with meat), it helps protect young arteries.*

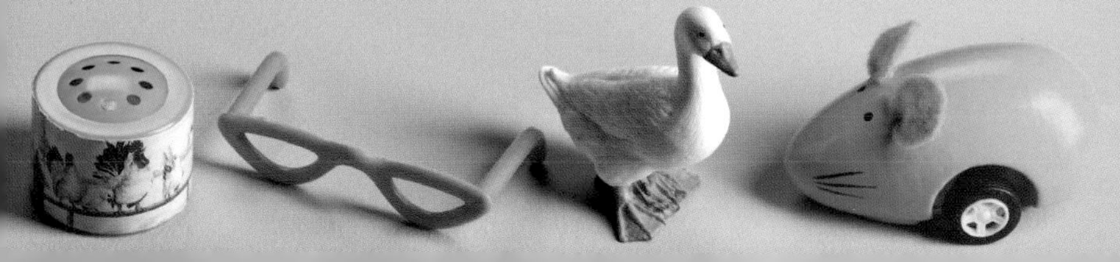

Let's Dive into Endives

… at the market: 2 endives - 1 sprig flat-leaf parsley - a few drops lemon juice

… at the grocery store: 2 Tbsp olive oil - 1 Tbsp balsamic vinegar - 1/4 turn of the pepper mill (white pepper) - 1 tiny pinch salt

scissors - cutting board - paring knife

Start by washing the parsley, removing the leaves, and cutting them up with scissors. Meticulously wash the endives. Remove the bitter white base and any damaged leaves with a knife. Keep 6 or 7 nice-looking raw leaves. With a knife, trim the edges so they look like feathers.

Cut the endives in half lengthwise. Place them in the steamer basket, sprinkle them with a few drops of lemon juice (to prevent them from turning brown), and cook them for 15 minutes (water level 3).

Make a balsamic vinaigrette (do not mix it though, so the oil beads on the vinegar). Add the chopped parsley to it. Season to taste.

When the endives are cooked, throw the cooking juices away and transfer the contents of the steamer basket to the blending bowl. Blend as gently as possible (1 pulse). Place this endive "cloud" at the center of the plate and pour the vinaigrette over it. Then place the endive "feathers" around it, just like a daisy.

GOOD POINTS: *Be it raw or cooked, the endive's soft fibers are easily tolerated by the digestive system of a young child. And this is in addition to its richness in water, minerals, trace elements, and folic acid (vitamin B9), which is of the utmost importance for the development of the nervous system.*

MORE WAYS TO LOVE IT: *Add a cooked quail's or chicken's egg to the plate to make a kid's steak and eggs! Make sure that your children don't have any nut allergies beforehand.*

And to mix things up, cut the potatoes into little pieces and pan-fry them (like in the photo).

3 years and up 25 mn

Mini-Filet of Beef and Pan-Fried Potatoes

… at the market: 1 small Yukon Gold potato - 3 fresh walnuts - 1 oz. bleu cheese - 1 Tbsp of heavy whipping cream - 50 g of beef (tenderloin tip)

… at the grocery store: 1 tablespoon of olive oil, 1 pat of butter

sharp non-serrated knife - 2 saucepans - slotted spoon small frying pan - nutcracker

Cut the meat into large chunks and place them in the blending bowl. Pulse 1 or 2 times to shred them. Shape into small patties with the hands.

Wash the potato, peel with the potato peeler and cut in half along its width. Place the two halves in a saucepan of cold water, then heat until boiling to blanch. Remove with a slotted spoon. Pour a little bit of olive oil into the frying pan and heat. Cook the potatoes until they are browned, then add butter and reduce heat.

While the potatoes are cooking, reduce the cream in a small saucepan: heat on low until the cream simmers. If you feel the cream is becoming too thick you can add a little water. Shell the nuts and place them in the blender with the cheese (cut into small pieces). Pulse twice. Add to the reduced cream and mix again (1 pulse).

When the potatoes are cooked (well browned), place them on the plate and cook the meat in the same pan. Set them on the side of the plate and drizzle the sauce over them.

12 months and up — 15 mn

Exotic Tastes Spécial

Pytt-i-Panna

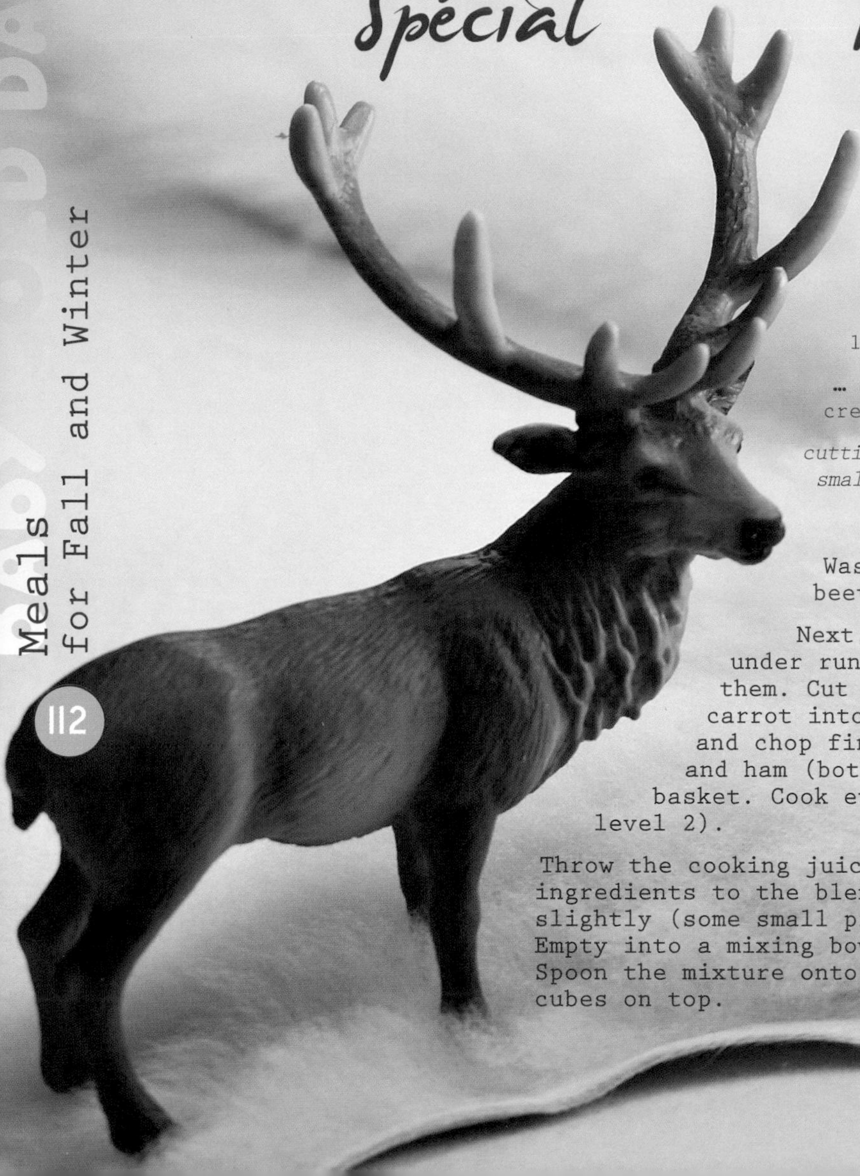

… at the market: 3 oz beef cut into large cubes - 1 slice smoked ham (0.75 oz) - 2 small Yukon Gold potatoes 1/4 onion - 1/2 carrot - 1/4 raw beet

… at the grocery store: 1 Tbsp heavy cream

cutting board - vegetable peeler - small knife - bowl

Wash, peel, and dice 1/4 of the raw beet. Set aside.

Next, rinse the other vegetables under running water, peel them, and wash them. Cut the two potatoes and the 1/2 carrot into small pieces. Peel the onion and chop finely. Place the vegetables, beef and ham (both cut into cubes) in the steamer basket. Cook everything for 10 minutes (water level 2).

Throw the cooking juices away. Transfer the cooked ingredients to the blending bowl. Pulse once to blend slightly (some small pieces should remain).
Empty into a mixing bowl and add the cream. Mix well.
Spoon the mixture onto a plate. Sprinkle the raw beet cubes on top.

GOOD POINTS: *In Sweden, Pytt-i-Panna is THE "dish for little boys." They love it because everything is cut into tiny bits. Protein from the beef, carbohydrates and fiber from the vegetables, calories from the small amount of smoked ham, and vitamin A from the cream. This recipe is definitely one that will chase away the winter blues!*

MORE WAYS TO LOVE IT: *When buying the beef, choose a topside beef cut into large cubes with a knife so that the pieces don't fall through the holes in the steamer basket.*

15 months and up · 25 mn

Exotic Tastes
Swedish Meatballs

… at the market: 1.5 oz minute steak - 1.5 oz lean pork belly - 1 "farm-fresh" free-range egg - 1 Tbsp thick crème fraîche - 2 small pats butter - 1 large new potato - 1/4 Spanish onion

… at the grocery store: 2 Tbsp prepared milk-based pediatric nutritional supplement - 1 tiny pinch salt - 1/4 turn of the pepper mill (white pepper)

small knife - cutting board - bowl - fork - wooden spoon - plastic wrap - vegetable peeler - 2 small mixing bowls - nonstick pan

To prepare the meat mixture, place the pieces of meat in the blending bowl. Pulse twice. Peel the onion, thinly slice 1/4 of it, and add it with the milk to the meat mixture. Break the egg into a bowl, beat it with a fork, and pour half of it into the blending bowl. Season very lightly.

Pulse once to obtain a homogenous mixture (or twice, stirring between pulses). Transfer to a mixing bowl, cover with plastic wrap, and let sit for 15 minutes in the refrigerator.

Wash the blending bowl, and prepare the side dish. Rinse the potato under running water, peel it with a vegetable peeler, wash it, and

cut it into small pieces. Place it in the steamer basket. Cook for 10 minutes (water level 2). Throw the cooking juices away. Transfer the potato to a mixing bowl, smash it with a fork, and add the crème fraîche and a small pat of butter. Mix. Keep warm.

Remove the meat mixture from the refrigerator and roll it between the palms of your hands into 4 or 5 meatballs the size of a chestnut. Melt a small pat of butter in a frying pan. As soon as it starts to bubble, place the meatballs in the pan and brown them on all sides.

Place the meatballs on the plate. Form the mashed potatoes into 2 dumplings with 2 soup spoons. Add them to the plate as a yummy decoration.

GOOD POINTS: *"Kött Bullar" (pronounced "schott boullar"!), or Swedish Meatballs, is a recipe made on the weekend in Sweden. This delicious dish is a treat for kids in the fall and warms them in the winter. And it's not surprising, with its many health benefits: the meatballs are loaded with protein (beef and pork, which are also good sources of iron), stuffed with vitamins (dairy), and full of calories (carbohydrates in the potatoes). And an egg, the perfect food, to boot.*

MORE WAYS TO LOVE IT: *Make sure the meat mixture spends enough time in the fridge! If the meat is cool, the meatballs will be easier to roll and won't fall apart in the frying pan. To save some time, ask the butcher to finely chop the meat with a knife right in front of you.*

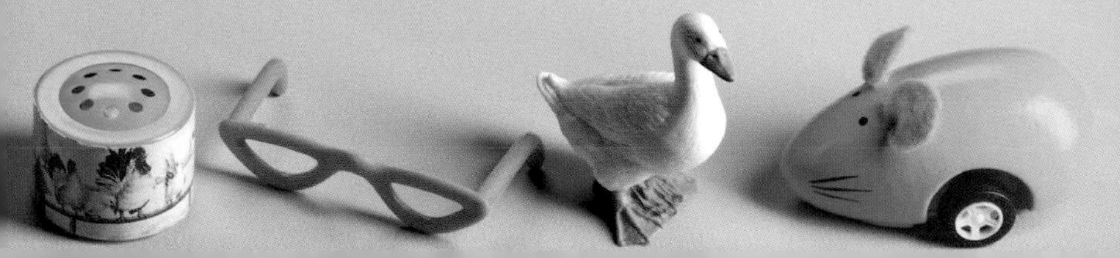

18 months and up 25 mn

Exotic Tastes

My First Couscous

… at the market: 0.75 oz carrot - 0.75 oz thin French-style green beans - 0.75 oz zucchini - 0.75 oz turnip - 0.75 oz celery root - 1 sprig fresh coriander - 2 mint leaves, 0.75 oz ground lamb (shoulder, neck, or leg) - 0.75 oz ground free-range chicken breast

… at the grocery store: 3 Tbsp (1 oz) medium-grain couscous semolina - 1 tsp olive oil - 1 pat butter

soup bowl - plastic wrap - cutting board - paring knife - mixing bowl

Prepare the couscous semolina. Place the couscous semolina in a soup bowl. Add enough hot water to cover the couscous grains, cover the bowl with plastic wrap, and allow it to rise.

Wash all the vegetables as well as the sprig of fresh coriander (but not the mint) and peel. Cut them into large pieces and place them in the steamer basket. Cook for 10 minutes (water level 2). Throw the cooking juices away. Add the ground meat, and cook for 5 more minutes.

While it is cooking, rip the 2 mint leaves into pieces. Use a fork to transfer the couscous semolina to a mixing bowl and break up the clumps. Add the butter, olive oil, and mint. Gently mix and set aside.

When the meat and vegetables are cooked, throw the cooking juices away. Transfer the cooked food to the blending bowl. Pulse once so that some pieces remain. If the pieces are too large for your child to chew, pulse once more.

Spoon the couscous semolina onto the plate, make a little well in the middle, and pour the sauce into it. Bon appétit!

GOOD POINTS: *This recipe wins the prize for most balanced meal: animal protein from the meat, vegetable protein from the vegetables (along with the complete array of essential amino acids), and carbohydrates from the couscous semolina. A well balanced meal.*

Exotic Tastes

Mary Had a Little Lamb (Kefta)

… at the market: 3 oz lamb (shoulder, neck or leg) - 1 sprig fresh coriander - 1/4 Spanish onion - 1 medium-sized baking potato

… at the grocery store: 1/2 tsp cumin powder - olive oil - 1 tsp tomato paste

cutting board - paring knife - small mixing bowl - plastic wrap - vegetable peeler - small saucepan - wooden spoon

Wash the fresh coriander under running water and remove the leaves. Peel the onion and cut it into quarters. Dice 1/4 of the onion.

Cut the lamb into large pieces and place them directly in the blending bowl. Add the olive oil, diced onion, fresh coriander leaves, and cumin. Pulse 3 times to obtain a smooth mixture. Transfer the mixture to a mixing bowl, cover with plastic wrap, and let rest in the refrigerator.

Prepare the sauce: Rinse the potato, peel it with a vegetable peeler, wash it, and dice it. Heat the olive oil and potatoes in a saucepan over low heat for 30 seconds without allowing it to brown. Add just enough water to cover the potatoes. Add the

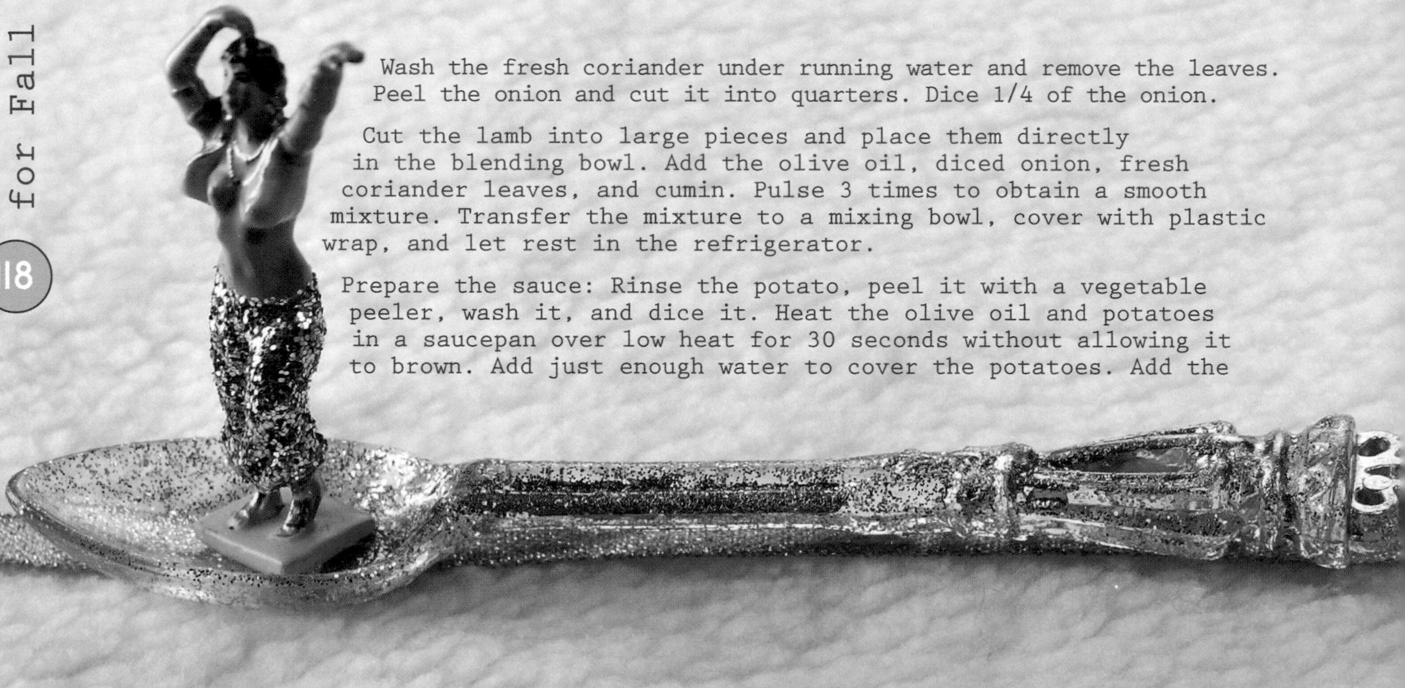

tomato paste and allow it to thicken while stirring gently. The sauce will turn an appetizing red color. Remove from heat.

Now it's time to make the lamb meatballs. Remove the meat mixture from the refrigerator. Roll it with the palms of your hands into 5 or 6 meatballs the size of a cherry. Drop the meatballs in the sauce and cook them for 6 or 7 minutes over low heat. Serve this mouth-watering meatball ragout when it is nice and red.

GOOD POINTS: *Baby will discover a new spice: cumin, which brings out the lamb's tenderness and flavor. This dish will stimulate his eyes and taste buds, as well as his curiosity and imagination.*

Meals for Special Days

Scallop Tartare

Beef Stroganoff

Sea Bass with Fennel

Fish Dumplings in Mushroom Sauce

Veal Cakes

Socca Nicoise

Tom, Tom the Turkey

Ham and Pumpkin Au Gratin

Ricotta Gnocchi

Mom Loves your Heart and Sole

Swiss Chard au Gratin

Salmon Brandade with Swiss Chard

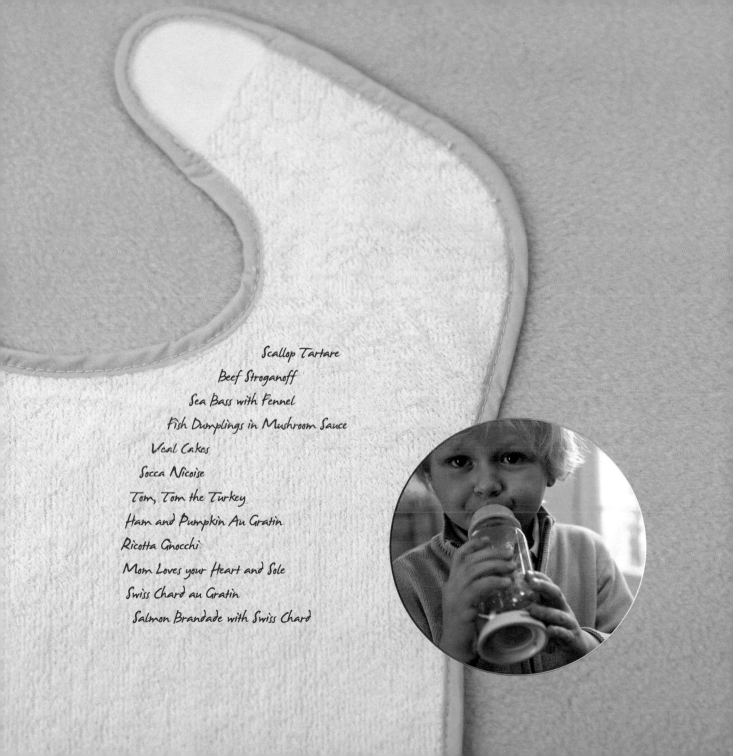

Scallop Tartare

… at the market: 2 nice-looking scallops (and their shells) - 1 blade chives - 1 shallot

… at the grocery store: 1 or 2 tiny, crunchy cornichons (French pickles) - 1/2 teaspoon capers - 1 thin drizzle olive oil - 1 tiny pinch salt - 1/4 turn of the pepper mill (white pepper)

pastry brush - paring knife - cutting board - bowl-spatula - mixing bowl

Carefully clean the scallops with a pastry brush under a trickle of water. Then wash the shells under running water.

Cut the cornichons and the shallot (you'll only use a pinch) into large pieces. Place the cornichons, shallot, and capers in the blending bowl. Pulse once. Place this mix in a bowl. Chop the chives with a knife and set aside.

Next, cut the scallops into small pieces and place them in the blending bowl. Pulse twice, stirring between the pulses to redistribute the pieces. Add the chives and the cornichon/caper/shallot mixture. Pulse once more.

Transfer the mixture to a mixing bowl. Lightly season to taste (just a little!). Add a thin drizzle of olive oil. Mix.

Spoon little piles of the scallop tartare onto the center of the shells.

MORE WAYS TO LOVE IT: *Frozen scallops are not good for tartares. Make sure to choose only the freshest scallops (alive, with a tightly closed shell, and odorless). Handle them as little as possible before preparing the recipe because they should be eaten raw.*

GOOD POINTS: *The flavor and firm flesh of Scallops will hook children right away and make them seafood fans for life. But wait for the right age. Their iodine content can provoke allergic reactions in little ones, so wait until your child is at least 18 months old before testing this delicacy out… using a sailor's caution.*

Beef Stroganoff

… at the market: 1 large agria potato - 1/4 carrot - 1/2 tomato (medium sized) - 1 handful of fresh peas (or frozen) 1/4 white onion - 3 oz. of finely chopped beef

… at the grocery store: 1 pinch of salt - 1 handful of ice cubes

For older children: 1/4 turn of the pepper mill (white pepper) - 1 pinch of paprika

cutting board - saucepan - slotted spoon - paring knife - vegetable peeler - 2 mixing bowls - plastic wrap

Place the ice cubes in a mixing bowl with a little water. Boil some water separately in a saucepan.

Wash the vegetables in running water, peel the carrot and potato with the vegetable peeler. Peel the tomato: this will be easier by soaking it in boiling water for 20 seconds and then transferring it to the bowl of ice water.

Cut the tomato and carrot in half. Use 1/2 of each.
Dice the tomato, carrot and potato. Wash and place in the steamer. Remove the onion's outer layer. Finely chop 1/4 of the onion and add to the steamer. Cook for 15 min (water level 3).

Throw away the cooking juices. Transfer vegetables to the blender and pulse once. Set aside in a salad bowl covered with plastic wrap.

Shell the peas and cook them "à l'anglaise" (in the saucepan of boiling salted water) for 30 seconds. Remove them using the slotted spoon and soak for a few seconds in the ice water in order to keep them green and firm.

Place the meat in the steamer (the little holes in the steamer pan should be smaller than the small pieces of meat) and cook for 5 min (water level 1). The meat should still be soft.

Mix the meat with the vegetables in a second mixing bowl, then pour into the little gourmet's plate. Lightly season and place the peas on top as decoration.

Add a trace of paprika to stimulate older children's taste buds.

GOOD POINTS: *This dish is a good source of protein (beef, peas) as well as iron! Beef is one of the best sources of iron (as well as zinc and vitamins PP and B12), provided the beef is freshly chopped and cooked within 3 hours. Peas from firm, crisp pods with a brilliant green color are rich in protein and carbohydrates and low in fat. Fresh or frozen, peas are a good source of fiber, vitamins A, C, B9 and iron.*

12 months and up · 20 mn

Sea Bass with Fennel

… at the market: 1 oz wild Atlantic sea bass - 1/4 fennel bulb - 1 small dried fennel stalk - 1/2 small plum tomato - 2 basil leaves - 3 drops lemon juice

… at the grocery store: 1 drizzle olive oil - 1 tiny pinch salt and a few ice cubes

cutting board - paring knife - 2 mixing bowls - small saucepan - wooden spoon

Wash the fennel bulb under running water and cut it into quarters. Cut one of the quarters into thin slices. Cut the sea bass filet into thin strips.

Place the sea bass and sliced fennel into the steamer basket. Cook for 15 minutes (water level 3).

Prepare a tomato vinaigrette:

Fill a mixing bowl with water and ice cubes. Boil a saucepan of water. Wash the tomato and stem it. Dip it into the boiling water for 30 seconds and then into the ice water before peeling it. The skin should come off very easily.

Wash the basil, remove the leaves from the stems, and rip the leaves into pieces. Cut the tomato into quarters, remove the seeds (it's easy to do with your thumb), and cut 2 of the quarters into small pieces. Mix the chopped tomato in a mixing bowl with the olive oil, salt, basil, and 3 drops of lemon juice (and no more!). Set aside.

Once the sea bass is cooked, throw the dried fennel stalk and cooking juices away. Transfer the sea bass and cooked fennel to the blending bowl. Pulse twice. Spoon the mixture onto a plate, and sprinkle with the tomato vinaigrette.

GOOD POINTS: *The subtle flavors will sharpen the taste buds. The delicate taste of the sea bass is brought out by the fennel, which is a "sweet dill" with an aniseed-like taste. Used dried and fresh, fennel is rich in sodium and calcium.*

MORE WAYS TO LOVE IT: *Choose wild Atlantic sea bass over its farmed cousin. The latter can be found more easily, but the flesh is much less tender because it has never swum in the sea!*

Fish Dumplings in Mushroom Sauce

For the dumplings

… at the market: 2 oz white meat fish: whiting, hake, sole, or pike - 2 Tbsp butter - 1 "farm-fresh" free-range egg - 1 Tbsp heavy cream

… at the grocery store: 1 tiny pinch salt - 1/4 turn of the pepper mill (white pepper)

For the sauce

… at the market: 2 oz button mushrooms (3.5 medium sized mushrooms) - 1 shallot - 1 sprig thyme - 2 Tbsp heavy cream - 1 pat butter

… at the grocery store: 1 tiny pinch salt - 1/4 turn of the pepper mill (white pepper)

2 small mixing bowls - plastic wrap - cutting board - 2 small saucepans - bowl - 2 spoons (size of spoons depends on the size of dumplings desired) - slotted spoon

Prepare the fish mixture first. Place the fish you have chosen into the blending bowl to chop it finely (1 pulse). Add the butter to the blending bowl. Break the egg into it. Pulse again. Add the cream, a bit of salt, and a very little bit of pepper. Pulse once more.

Taste to see if there is enough salt and add more, if necessary. Transfer the mixture to a mixing bowl, cover with plastic wrap, and place it in the refrigerator. Wash the blending bowl.

Make the mushroom sauce. To prepare the mushrooms, remove the dirty end of their stems, wash them twice in a big bowl of cool water,

and cut them in half. Peel the shallot and chop it finely. Warm a pat of butter in a saucepan over low heat. Sweat the shallot and mushrooms in it for 30 seconds without browning them. Add the cream, the thyme, and a little salt. Cook for 5 minutes. Remove the sprig of thyme. Transfer the contents of the saucepan to the blending bowl and pulse 3 times. Salt to taste. Set aside.

Now make the dumplings: heat a saucepan of salted water without allowing it to boil. Remove the fish mixture from the refrigerator. Use 2 spoons (that you've dipped in the hot water so the mixture won't stick to them) to form large or small dumplings, depending on the spoons you have chosen. Use the slotted spoon to place them in the hot water to cook. Cook them for 2 minutes (for large dumplings) and then remove them with the slotted spoon.

Place the dumplings in the soup bowl and cover them with the mushroom sauce.

GOOD POINTS: *An introduction to a professional chef's recipe, with the freedom for artists to let their creativity flow when making the dumplings (into the shape of a little white mouse, for example!). And the assurance that baby is getting all the virtues the sea has to offer, even if he or she does not like fish…dumplings melt in your mouth, and who doesn't like that!*

MORE WAYS TO LOVE IT: *Choose whichever fish you like, as long as it is white, thin, and extremely fresh. Ask your fishmonger to bone it. To save time, you can make the fish mixture and the sauce the night before. Then all you have to do is reheat the sauce and cook the dumplings right before suppertime!*

12 months and up · 30 mn

Veal Cakes and Button Mushroom Purée

… at the market: 1 oz veal loin (from a calf raised by its mother, if possible) - 2 sprigs flat-leaf parsley - 1 tsp heavy cream - 2 "farm-fresh" free-range chicken eggs - 1 small pat butter

… at the grocery store: 1 rounded Tbsp flour - 3 Tbsp breadcrumbs - 1 Tbsp grapeseed oil - 1 tiny pinch salt - 1/4 turn of the pepper mill (white pepper)

scissors - cutting board - knife - small mixing bowl - plastic wrap - 3 bowls - fork - nonstick pan

Start by preparing the meat mixture. Wash the parsley under running water and shake it well. Remove the leaves from the stem and cut them up with scissors. Dice the veal and place it in the blending bowl along with the parsley and heavy cream. Add the egg as well. Pulse 3 times, stirring between each pulse with a spatula to obtain a fine, dense mixture. Season lightly. Transfer the mixture to a mixing bowl, cover with plastic wrap, and let rest in the refrigerator for 15 to 20 minutes.

Line 3 bowls up in a row. Place the flour in the first bowl. Break an egg in the second and beat it. Place the breadcrumbs in the third.

When the meat mixture is cool, form it into little "pucks" (flattened meatballs) with the palms of your hands. Pick up each puck with a fork and dip it in the flour, then in the egg, and finally in

the breadcrumbs, tapping it each time on the edge of the bowl to remove any excess ingredient. Set the pucks aside.

Heat a small pat of butter and a tablespoon of grapeseed oil in a frying pan over medium heat. When it starts to bubble, reduce the heat, and brown the pucks on both sides. And the veal cakes are ready to crunched on by little chompers! Served with the Button Mushroom Purée (see page 55).

18 months and up — 15 to 20 mn

Socca niçoise

… at the grocery store: 5.5 tbsp chickpea flour - 1 drizzle of olive oil

small saucepan - measuring cup - whisk - small pie pan

Preheat the oven to 425 °F (gas 7).

Heat 1/2 cup of water in a small saucepan.

When it starts to simmer, sprinkle 1/2 cup (about 1.5 oz) of chickpea flour into the saucepan and beat it vigorously to obtain a dough. Cook for 3 or 4 minutes. When it becomes unstuck from the saucepan, place it in the blending bowl with a drizzle of olive oil

Blend to rid the dough of all lumps (3 pulses). Spread it out in a pie pan and place it in the oven for 5 minutes.

GOOD POINTS: *It's very simple and oh so good, and the chickpea brings along its calories, proteins, carbohydrates, fiber and vitamins!*

MORE WAYS TO LOVE IT: *The socca's success depends on how it is cooked: the dough should be flaky on the outside and gooey on the inside.*

MORE WAYS TO LOVE IT: *Choose a green, full cabbage with curly leaves and white turkey meat. The very small amount of smoked country bacon helps bring out the dish's flavor.*

Tom, Tom the Turkey

… at the market: 1 small Savoy cabbage - 1.75 oz turkey breast - 1 small slice smoked country bacon (0.75 oz)

… at the grocery store: 1 small pat butter - 1 tiny pinch salt - 1/4 turn of the pepper mill (white pepper)

cutting board - small knife - bowl

Prepare the cabbage by removing its first layer of leaves, which pull away easily. Remove the core with a knife. Cut the cabbage into quarters and use only one. Wash it in a large bowl of water with a teaspoon of vinegar. Cut the leaves into strips that are not too thin and place them in the steamer basket.

Thinly slice the turkey meat and bacon. Add them to the steamer basket with the butter. Cook everything for 15 minutes (water level 3). Throw the cooking juices away.

Spoon onto a plate and lightly season with salt (not too much because the bacon is already salty!) and pepper. Taste and add more, if necessary. Serve as is.

GOOD POINTS: *When baby discovers the pieces of turkey hidden in the tender cabbage leaves, it helps him to develop a taste for two different flavors and two consistencies. Plus, baby will get his fill of vitamin C (to strengthen his body's defenses) and protein in a hearty winter meal.*

8 months and up — 30 mn

Ham and Pumpkin Au Gratin

GOOD POINTS:
Sweet tastes, harmonious colors, playful consistencies… The ham-pumpkin combination is particularly good at seducing wary little ones into trying new things, and at nourishing their little bodies with the minerals found in pumpkin (extremely rich in potassium) and the protein found in high-quality boiled ham, which is just as good as the protein found in red meat.

… at the market: 5.25 oz prepared pumpkin (= 1 medium-sized slice) - 3 oz boiled ham, thick slices (1/4 inch thick) - 0.75 oz fresh Parmesan - 1 generous-sized pat butter

… at the grocery store: 3 good-sized Tbsp prepared milk-based pediatric nutritional supplement (or prepared baby formula for 8 to 12-month-old babies) - 1 tiny pinch salt - 1/4 turn of the pepper mill (white pepper)

cutting board - paring knife - cheese grater - bowl - ramekin

Start by cutting the fat off the ham. Cut the ham into tiny pieces (watch your fingers!), grate the Parmesan (1 tablespoon), and set both of them aside. Prepare the pumpkin. Wash it, remove the rind and seeds, cut the flesh into pieces, and place them directly in the steamer basket with a tiny pinch of salt. Cook for 15 minutes (water level 3). Preheat the broiler.Pour the cooking juices into a bowl. Place the cooked pumpkin in the blending bowl with the milk and butter. Pulse 3 times to obtain a smooth, liquid consistency. If necessary, add a small amount of cooking juices (1 tablespoon at most) between 2 pulses. Transfer to the mixing bowl. Add the ham pieces, a bit of salt, and a tiny bit of pepper. Mix well and pour into the ramekin. Sprinkle with the grated Parmesan. Broil for 10 minutes for a sunny-colored gratin.

GOOD POINTS: *Ricotta is made with goat's or sheep's milk from the region of Campania in Italy. It is used in desserts such as pastaria, a tart covered with sugared fruits made to celebrate Easter in Naples. Nutmeg comes from Indonesia, where it is known for its sedative effects. Just take 2 drops of nutmeg oil in a glass of warm milk!*

MORE WAYS TO LOVE IT: *Add a little extra salt when your child is older. When he is nearing 3 years add a little bit of pepper. You can replace the Ricotta with curdled sheep's milk, which is sweeter, and serve it with the Spinach Purée (p. 107).*

12 months and up 15 mn

Ricotta Gnocchi

… at the market: 1 extra-fresh free-range egg - 9 oz. (about 1 cup) ricotta

… at the grocery store: 5.5 tbsp flour - 1 tsp olive oil - 1 pinch of ground nutmeg - 1 pinch of fleur de sel - a tiny bit of pepper for older children

small saucepan - slotted spoon - paring knife - glass or bowl

To make the gnocchi dough, cut the cheese into small pieces and place in the mixer with the egg, flour, olive oil and nutmeg. Pulse 3 times.

Dip a teaspoon in hot water and use it to shape the dough into several olive-sized gnocchi. Re-dip the spoon each time so the dough does not stick.

Heat a saucepan of water. When it boils, poach the gnocchi for 30 to 40 seconds and remove from the water with the slotted spoon. They are done when they float to the surface.

Eat immediately with a little olive oil and a pinch of fleur de sel.

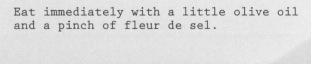

Mom Loves your Heart and Sole

… at the market: 2 filets sole - 5 cups (5 oz) fresh spinach - 1/2 lemon

… at the grocery store: 1 pinch salt - 2 pats butter - a few ice cubes

cutting board - plastic wrap - paring knife - mixing bowl - saucepan - slotted spoon - 2 toothpicks

Flatten the sole filets (without smashing them!) by covering them with a sheet of plastic wrap, lightly moistening it, and pressing them down with the flat edge of a knife.

Fill a mixing bowl with cool water and ice cubes. Place a saucepan of salted water on to boil.

Stem the spinach leaves by hand. Wash them thoroughly, changing the water several times. Blanch them for 30 seconds in boiling water and then plunge them in the ice water (to preserve their bright green color). Remove them with a slotted spoon and gently squeeze them with your hands to remove any excess water.

Sprinkle the sole filets with salt and butter them with a knife. Place a layer of spinach on top of each filet, and then roll the filets. Pierce them with a toothpick to hold the rolls together. Place both rolls in the steamer basket and cook for 7 to 8 minutes (water level slightly above 1). When they are cooked, cut them in slices.

And voila! Beautiful multi-colored spirals! Place the half lemon on the edge of the plate to squeeze a few drops of lemon on each slice.

GOOD POINTS: *A balanced dish that combines essential fatty acids from a lean white fish with all the rich minerals of a green, leafy vegetable. Fresh sole is tender (it is drier when bought frozen) and spinach melts in your mouth. A playful combination to help little ones accept this veggie that is often pushed away…*

MORE WAYS TO LOVE IT:
Buy a very fresh small sole from your fishmonger and have him bone it.

10 months and up — 25 mn

Swiss Chard Au Gratin

… at the market: 2 leaves of Swiss chard (with whites) - 1/2 seedless lemon - .5 oz. Parmesan

… at the grocery store: 1 teaspoon of liquid crème fraiche - 1 pinch of salt - 1/4 turn of the pepper mill (white pepper)

vegetable peeler - paring knife - cutting board - mixing bowl - 2 saucepans - au gratin dishes

Fill the mixing bowl with water and a few drops of lemon juice. Preheat the oven to broil.

Separate the green and white of the chard. Use a potato peeler to peel the whites and remove all of the strings. Cut into small cubes and put them in the mixing bowl filled with lemon water (to keep them from discoloring). Let them sit in the water for a few minutes then put them in the steamer. Cook for 15 minutes (water level 3).

Wash the greens under running water and cut into strips. Boil a saucepan of salted water. Boil the greens for 3 or 4 seconds, remove with a slotted spoon and drain by pressing on them softly.

In the second saucepan, mix the cooked cubes of chard white and the greens over low heat, slowly adding the cream, salt, and pepper. When it’s hot, transfer into the small au gratin dishes. Sprinkle with parmesan and broil for 5 min.

MORE WAYS TO LOVE IT: Replace the Parmesan with other grated cheeses like Comté or Cantal, Beaufort or Abondance.

GOOD POINTS: *Swiss chard is rich in fiber and (though few realize it) vitamin C, beta carotene, potassium and calcium. It contains very few carbohydrates, but it does have iron.*

MORE WAYS TO LOVE IT: *You can substitute cod for salmon, thus making the dish one step closer to a true brandade.*

GOOD POINTS: *This dish unites a "cold water fish," rich in essential fatty acids, and a vegetable straight from our gardens whose qualities are not always recognized. Together, they are a gold mine of valuable minerals and the vitamins the body needs to assimilate them.*

10 months and up 20 mn

Salmon Brandade with Swiss Chard

… at the market: 3 oz wild salmon filet - 1 large Yukon Gold potato - 2 leaves French Swiss Chard - 1 sprig thyme - 1 garlic clove

… at the grocery store: 2 Tbsp prepared milk-based pediatric nutritional supplement - 1 Tbsp breadcrumbs - 1 small pat butter - 1 tiny pinch salt

small gratin dish - cutting board - paring knife - vegetable peeler - saucepan - slotted spoon - mixing bowl - fork

Preheat the broiler. Butter the gratin dish.

Separate the green part of the Swiss chard leaves from the white (which we won't use in this recipe). Wash the green part under running water and cut it into strips. Rinse the potato in water, peel it, wash it, and dice it. Place the vegetables in the steamer basket and cook for 10 minutes (water level 2).

Pour the milk into a saucepan and add the thyme and unpeeled garlic clove. Warm over low heat. When the milk starts to simmer, add the salmon, and turn off the heat. Poach the salmon for no more than 5 minutes so that it remains tender. Remove the salmon with a slotted spoon. Place it in a mixing bowl, break it up with a fork, and set it aside.

When the vegetables are cooked, throw the cooking juices away, and transfer the vegetables to the blending bowl. Pulse 3 times. Mix the salmon with the vegetables. Season to taste with a tiny bit of salt, if necessary. Transfer the mixture to the gratin dish. Sprinkle some breadcrumbs over top and brown under the broiler for 5 minutes.

SWEETS FOR BABY

Sweets for Baby
Desserts, Snacks, Tea-time

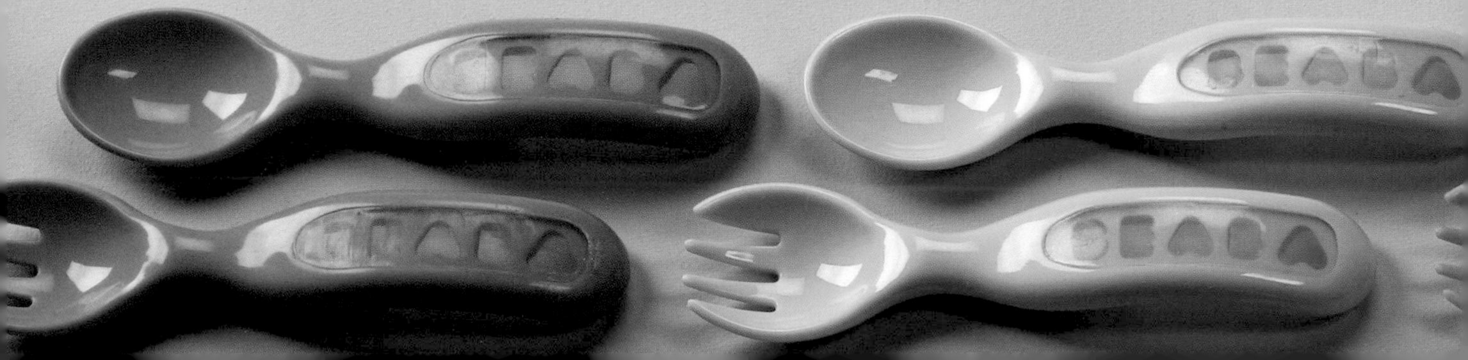

Yogourt Shakes à la Carte (5)

Langues de Chat

Banana Yogurt with Honey

Cherry Granité

Watermelon Granité

Strawberry Rhubarb Crumble

Fromage Blanc with Walnuts

Madeleines

Quince Compote

Vanilla Peach Compote

Cinnamini cookies (Pepparkakor)

Chocolate Cookies

Mango Hedgehog and Marmalade

Cherry Clafouti

Candlemas Crêpes

Pancakes à l'orange

BEABA

6 months and up — 5 mn

Yogurt Shakes
à la carte

… basic ingredients: 1 "just for baby" yogurt for children 6-12 months old or 1 yogurt made with whole milk for children over 1 - 1 tablespoon crushed ice

small knife - cutting board - shatterproof glass

Strawberry-Banana Yogurt Shake

… at the market: 1/2 large ripe banana

For children over one year: 1 dozen strawberries

… at the grocery store: about 1 teaspoon sugar

Wash the strawberries, stem them, and cut them in half.

Peel the banana and cut it into slices. Place the fruit in the blending bowl. Blend slightly (1 short pulse).

Add the yogurt, crushed ice, and sugar. Pulse once more. Pour into a glass and serve.

GOOD POINTS: *A great pair, but make sure your child isn't allergic to strawberries! The consistency is a winner: babies love bananas. The nutritional values are rich: the starch and potassium found in bananas compliment the vitamin C in strawberries.*

Strawberry-Kiwi Yogurt Shake

… at the market: 1 small ripe kiwi

For children over one year: 1 dozen strawberries

… at the grocery store: about 1 tsp sugar

Wash the strawberries, stem them, and cut them in half.

Wash and peel the kiwi, and cut in slices.
Place the fruit in the blending bowl. Blend slightly (1 short pulse).

Add the yogurt, crushed ice, and a little sugar.
Pulse once more.

Taste and add a bit more sugar, if necessary.
Pour into a glass and serve.

GOOD POINTS: *Loaded with vitamins and vitality, and dominated by vitamin C. And of course, test for a strawberry allergy before allowing baby to enjoy.*

Raspberry Yogurt Shake

… at the market: 0.33 oz ripe raspberries (6 berries)

… at the grocery store: about 1 teaspoon sugar

Carefully wash the raspberries and place them in the blending bowl. Blend slightly (1 short pulse).

Add the yogurt, crushed ice, and a little sugar (very little if the raspberries are very ripe). Pulse once more.

Taste and add a bit more sugar, if necessary. Pour into a glass and serve.

GOOD POINTS: *A pretty pink color, and a good dose of vitamin C.*

Blackcurrant Yogurt Shake

… at the market: 2 Tbsp blackcurrants

… at the grocery store: about 1 teaspoon sugar

Wash the blackcurrants and place them in the blending bowl. Blend slightly (1 pulse). Add the yogurt, crushed ice, and a bit of sugar. Pulse once more.

Taste and add a bit more sugar, if necessary. Pour into a glass and serve.

GOOD POINTS: *It is said that blackcurrants keep their vitamin C no matter how they are prepared, which is very important in cold winter months!*

Fig-Honey Yogurt Shake

… at the market: 1 nice-looking, ripe fig

… at the grocery store: 1 Tbsp white honey

Wash the fig, peel it, and cut it into small pieces. Place them in the blending bowl. Pulse once.

Add the yogurt, crushed ice, and honey. Pulse once more.

Pour into a glass and serve.

GOOD POINTS: *A good fall recipe that is extremely nourishing and should be reserved for young athletes 3 and up. Figs are rich in sugar (and valued for their fiber), and so is honey.*

Langues de chat

… at the grocery store: 3.8 oz. butter - 2.5 oz. egg white (about 2 large egg whites) from a free-range chicken - 1/2 cup sifted flour - 5.5 Tbsp confectioner's sugar

small saucepan - wooden spoon - mixing bowl - plastic wrap - paring knife - oven rack - cookie sheet - bowl

Melt the butter in the saucepan over very low heat. Pour into the blender.

Add the confectioner's sugar and the sifted flower. Pulse 1 time.

Add the egg white little by little. Pulse 1 or 2 times. Make sure the mixture is very smooth.

Pour into a mixing bowl. Cover with plastic wrap and place in the refrigerator for 10 min.

Pre-heat the oven to 400° F (gas 6). Cover the cookie sheet with a silicone baking sheet or baking paper.

Once it has rested, use a teaspoon to shape the dough into little domes on a cookie sheet. Space them about 2 inches apart.

Put the cookie sheet in the oven and reduce the oven temperature to 340° F (gas 4). Remove after about 10 minutes, when the cookies have browned around the edges.

MORE WAYS TO LOVE IT: *Langue de Chat goes well with desserts that children enjoy. You can dip them in hot chocolate when the little ones are old enough.*

12 months and up · 5 mn

Banana Yogurt with Honey

… at the market: 1 well ripened banana - 1 cup of plain yogurt or petit-suisse for babies

… at the grocery store: 1 tsp honey (acacia)

fork - bowl - spatula

Remove the peel from the banana and cut it into small pieces. Place in the mixer. Pulse 2 times for very little children, 1 time for older children.

Pour into a bowl. Add the yogurt and the honey and mix well. That's it!

GOOD POINTS: *An easy recipe that gives kids lots of calories. Banana and honey, a combination kids love!*

MORE WAYS TO LOVE IT: *Smash the banana with a fork! As the baby gets older, you can leave some little pieces in. Even if your baby doesn't have teeth yet, he will love "chewing" the little bits of banana.*

12 months and up · 10 mn + 30 mn

Cherry Granité

GOOD POINTS: *A light and easily digestible recipe that is cool, sweet, and restorative, too, because cherries are revitalizing. As easy to make as it is to eat…but be careful, because cherry juice can stain! You can also scoop this granité on top of a cherry clafouti (p. 173), for an unexpected and playful "raw on cooked" dessert.*

… at the market: 7 oz dark sweet cherries - 2 or 3 drops of lemon juice

… at the grocery store: 1/2 cup (3.33 oz) slightly mineralized water - 1 Tbsp fine sugar

dish towel - cherry pitter - paring knife - small saucepan - wooden spoon - fork - small bowl (approximately 4 inches)

Wash the cherries under running water. Towel dry. Stem them and pit them with a cherry pitter.

Place them in the blending bowl. Pulse just once to blend and to keep small pieces of fruit, too.

Pour the water and sugar into a saucepan. Cook over low heat until the mixture boils. Remove from heat, and mix 2 or 3 drops of lemon juice and the blended cherries into the sugar syrup.

Pour the mixture into a bowl and place it in the freezer. Leave it there for at least 30 minutes. Remove it and scrape with a fork to obtain small chips of granité ice.

8 months and up 10 mn + 30 mn

Watermelon Granité

… at the market: 1 slice of watermelon - 2 or 3 drops of lemon

… at the grocery store: 3.4 fl oz. slightly mineralized water - 4 tsp fine sugar

paring knife - small saucepan - wooden spoon - fork - small bowl (approximately 4 inches)

Use 1 slice of watermelon. Cut the fruit from its rind and remove the seeds. Cut it into pieces. Pulse once.

Pour the water and sugar into a saucepan over low heat. Remove from heat when the mixture reaches a boil and mix in the watermelon and 2 or 3 drops of lemon juice.

Pour into a glass and place in the freezer for 30 minutes (minimum), remove and scrape with a fork before serving to obtain the “gratiné” effect.

GOOD POINTS: A pretty, refreshing dessert with plenty of water to keep kids hydrated on hot summer days.

3 years and up — 40 mn + 1 hour

Strawberry-Rhubarb Crumble

… at the market: 5.75 oz ripe strawberries - 5.25 oz rhubarb

… at the grocery store: 1 cup brown sugar - 1/2 cup almond powder - 3.5 Tbsp butter - 1/3 cup sifted flour

3 small mixing bowls - plastic wrap - bowl - paring knife - parchment paper - baking sheet - small, clear cup

Place the (softened) butter, almond powder, flour, and 1/4 cup of the sugar in the blending bowl. Pulse twice to obtain a moist, grainy dough. Transfer the dough to a mixing bowl, cover with plastic wrap, and let it rest for about an hour in the refrigerator.

Wash the blending bowl and preheat the oven to 350 °F (gas 5).

Wash the strawberries under running water, stem them, and place them in the steamer basket. Sprinkle them with some of the sugar (1/3 cup). Cook for 10 minutes (water level 2). Set the cooking juices aside in a bowl and transfer the strawberries to the blending bowl. Add a very small amount of the cooking juices. Pulse once to obtain a marmalade-like mixture. Pour into a mixing bowl and allow to cool for about 15 minutes in the refrigerator.

Wash the rhubarb stalks under running water and peel them (make sure to remove the stringy fibers). Cut the stalks into small pieces and place them in the steamer basket with the remaining sugar (2/3 cup). Cook for 15 minutes (water level 3). Transfer the rhubarb to the blending bowl, along with 1 tablespoon of the cooking juices. Pulse once to obtain a marmalade-like mixture. Pour it into a mixing bowl and allow it to cool for about 15 minutes in the refrigerator.

Lower the oven temperature to 300 °F (gas 3). Line the baking sheet with a sheet of parchment paper. Remove the dough from the refrigerator and crumble it onto the baking sheet. Place in the oven and bake for 20 minutes. Remove from the oven and allow to cool.

Spoon a layer of strawberry jam (2 tablespoons) and a layer of rhubarb jam (2 tablespoons) into a small, clear cup, and repeat. Then sprinkle with the crumble.

MORE WAYS TO LOVE IT:

Make sure that the sweet taste of the strawberries is stronger than the acidic taste of the rhubarb.
To change things up, substitute 5.75 onces of wild strawberries or of rasberries for the strawberries.

MORE WAYS TO LOVE IT: *To give a little flavor back to the dried nuts, soak them (without shells) in milk for a few hours before preparing. As for the honey, we choose acacia honey for its refined, light aroma. You can substitute ground cinnamon (about half a teaspoon) for a more accentuated flavor.*

3 years and up — 5 mn

Fromage blanc with Walnuts

… at the market: 6 dried walnuts (3 fresh nuts with shell) - 4 tsp fromage blanc (20% milk fat) - a pinch of salt

… at the grocery store: 1 tbsp acacia honey

nut-cracker small dish

Crack open the 3 nuts and remove the 6 kernels.

Place five of the kernels in the mixer to break them into small pieces (2 pulses)

Add the fromage blanc. Pulse once.

Pour into a small bowl with the last whole walnut floating in the middle. Drizzle with the honey.

GOOD POINTS: *This dish helps to build strong little bodies because it mixes animal proteins from the fromage blanc (as well as its calcium and iron) with vegetable proteins from the walnuts (and their essential fatty acids). Also, dried nuts have more calories than fresh nuts. Always make sure that your child does not have any nut allergies.*

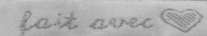

15 months and up — 45 mn

Madeleines

MORE WAYS TO LOVE IT:
Replace the lemon zest with a crushed vanilla bean to give your little one a nice surprise. And what should you do with the left over egg white? Make meringue! On the same day, of course!

… at the market: 2 "farm-fresh" free-range eggs - 1 egg yolk

… at the grocery store: 1/3 cup sugar - 1/2 cup sifted flour - 1 tsp baking powder - 2.6 oz. soft butter - 1 pinch of salt - zest from 1/4 lemon (shredded) - 1 pat of butter - 1 tsp of flour for the mold (if it is not non-stick)

grater - 2 bowls - small plate - mixing bowl - plastic wrap - baking sheet - silicon madeleine mold

Preheat the oven to 410° F (gas 6). Grate the skin of 1/4 lemon onto a small plate. Crack the two whole eggs into one bowl. Separate the white from a third egg into a separate bowl and cover with plastic wrap and place in the refrigerator. Place the yolk in the first bowl with the two whole eggs. Place the contents of your first bowl in the blender with sugar. Pulse 1 time. Add flour and baking powder and pulse 1 time. Add the butter and lemon zest and pulse once more. Transfer into a mixing bowl and cover with plastic wrap. Allow mixture to sit in the refrigerator for 15 min. When cooled, place 1 tsp of the mixture into each mold. Place the mold in the oven on a baking sheet. When the madeleines begin to rise, decrease the temperature to 320° (gas 4) and allow to cook for 20 more minutes then remove from oven. Remove the madeleines from the mold and allow to cool.

GOOD POINTS: *This delicacy has concentrated animal (egg) and vegetable (baking powder) proteins, carbohydrates (flour), and vitamins A (butter), B (baking powder) and C (lemon). The snack of champions! The quality of madeleines depends on how they are cooked. You should watch them closely. If you forget to reduce the oven temperature on time they will rise so much that they'll overflow the mold.*

10 months and up

20 mn

Quince Compote

… at the market: 1 slightly ripened quince - a few drops of lemon juice

… at the grocery store: 1 tsp sugar

cutting board - paring knife - bowl

Wash and peel the quince. Cut into quarters. Remove the core and seeds.

Coat the quarters with lemon juice so they don't brown. Cut into small pieces.

Place in the steamer with the sugar and 2 or 3 drops of lemon juice. Cook for 15 min (water level 3).

Save the cooking juices in a bowl and transfer the fruit to the blender. Pulse 3 times, adding a little of the cooking juices between each pulse to obtain a smooth texture.

GOOD POINTS: *The quince, rich in soft fiber, is as important as rice or carrots for taking care of the intestines. Little gourmets appreciate it because it is only used in sweet dishes, like this one.*

MORE WAYS TO LOVE IT: *Serve the quince compote as a dessert and the cooking juices as a snack in a bottle. Serve with gingerbread for older children!*

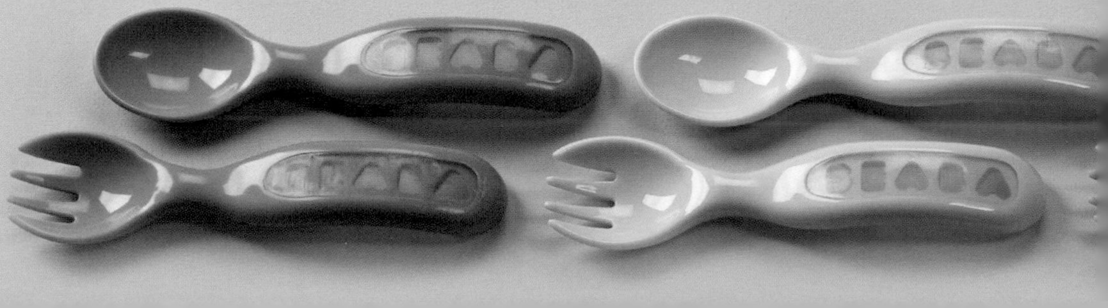

6 months and up 25 mn

GOOD POINTS: A refreshing recipe for hot weather. Its cooked fruit aids the digestive system, plus there is a duet of exotic flavors which brings out the taste of the peach: vanilla from Madagascar or Australia and (a more daring flavor, but one to try little by little), pepper from Malysia (a discreet flavor which future gourmets often enjoy).

Vanilla Peach Compote

… at the market: 2 ripe yellow peaches

… at the grocery store: 1 vanilla pod - 2 black pepper seeds - 1 oz sugar

paring knife - 2 bowls - a piece of cloth (linen, cheesecloth, jute) cooking twine

Make a little bag with the cloth and place the pepper seeds inside. Tie up with the string. Wash the peaches in running water and peel. Cut each peach into quarters and remove the pit. Place the fruit in the steamer and put the vanilla pod and the cloth bag with the pepper on top. Cook for 15 min (water level 3). When finished, open the vanilla pod with a knife and remove the pulp with a spoon. Save it in a bowl. Save the cooking juices in another bowl and remove the pepper. Transfer the fruit into the blender and sprinkle with sugar. Add a very small amount of the pulp from the vanilla pod. Pulse once. Taste to see if the vanilla flavor is sufficient. If it is not, add a little bit more of the pulp. For younger babies, add some of the cooking juices and pulse 1 more time to make the compote smooth. Serve hot or cold.

MORE WAYS TO LOVE IT: Be careful with the vanilla. It should support the flavor of the peach but not overwhelm it. Try this recipe with other fruits, like pears. You can also replace the peaches with apples and garnish with little pastries.

Cinnamini Cookies (Pepparkakor)

… at the market: 1 Tbsp ground cinnamon - 1/2 teaspoon clove powder - 1/2 teaspoon ginger powder - 1/2 cup butter - 2 "farm-fresh" free-range eggs - 1/2 Tbsp thick crème fraîche

… at the grocery store: 1 Tbsp sifted flour - 2 Tbsp sugar

mixing bowl - plastic wrap - silicon baking mat or parchment paper - baking sheet - daisy-shaped cookie cutter - pastry board

Prepare the dough. Place the flour, sugar, and butter in the blending bowl. Pulse twice. Add the crème, spices, and eggs and pulse twice more. Transfer the dough to a mixing bowl and cover it with plastic wrap. Let the dough rest for about 3 hours in the refrigerator.

While the dough is resting, preheat the oven to 400 °F (gas 6). Place the silicon baking mat or parchment paper on a baking sheet.

Roll the dough out so on a pastry board to a thickness of 1/8 to 1/4 inch.

Cut out the dough with the cookie cutter and place the cookies directly onto the silicon baking mat (or parchment paper). Reduce the oven temperature to 350 °F (gas 5). Place the baking sheet in the oven and bake for 15 minutes.

Let cool before tasting.

GOOD POINTS: *Round and daisy-shaped, thin, and light: these Pepparkakor (pronounced "pepacoca") are the favorite cookies of Swedish kids! You can add their many virtues to their "taste of Scandinavian heather: cinnamon calms the digestive tract, ginger aids digestion, and cloves soothe toothaches and stimulate the appetite.*

MORE WAYS TO LOVE IT: *In Sweden, these dry cookies are served with a glass of "Fläder Saft," a mixture of elderberry and blueberry syrup, which is both sweet and bitter and should be served very fresh, with water.*

GOOD POINTS: *A snack for the kids on days when they're fundled up to the ears! This recipe is adaptable: it can be made with or without nuts, with or whitout chocolate (white or dark), without either, or with both!*

MORE WAYS TO LOVE IT: *A recipe that can be adapted to your children's age and tastes (make sure your child has no nut allergies). Serve the cookies with a yogurt shake (page 146). They go together so well!*

3 years and up 30 mn

Chocolate Cookies

… at the market: 3/4 cup (3 oz) macadamia nuts - 2 farm-fresh, free-range eggs

… at the grocery store: 1 cup sifted flour - 2/3 cup brown sugar - 5 oz dark or white chocolate - 6 Tbsp butter - 1 teaspoon salt

paring knife - bowl - baking sheet - silicon baking mat or parchment paper - cutting board

Take the butter out of the refrigerator

Preheat the oven to 250 °F (gas 2). Line a baking sheet with a silicone baking mat or a piece of parchment paper.

Place the walnuts in the blending bowl. Pulse twice. Transfer the "crumbs" to a bowl.

Cut (or break) the chocolate into big pieces.

Place the butter (softened and cut into pieces), salt and sugar into the blending bowl and pulse twice. Add the flour and pulse twice more.

Add the eggs and pulse twice more. Transfer to a mixing bowl and mix in the chocolate and/or nuts.

Use your hands to shape the dough into little 1.5 inch long rolls (about the width of a walnut) to be flattened. Place the slices on the silicon baking mat or parchment paper on the baking sheet. Increase the oven temperature to 400 °F (gas 6). Bake for approximately 15 minutes. When they are golden, take them out of the oven and place them on a plate to harden. Serve warm, while the chocolate is still melting. Yum!

GOOD POINTS: *Fun to look at, easy to make, delicious to eat, easy to digest, and good for the body. Good for body and soul!*

MORE WAYS TO LOVE IT: *Why yellow mangoes from South-East Asia? Because they are the most flavorful, and flavor and consistency are of the essence of this recipe for 2 desserts. Twice the fun!*

12 months and up · 15 mn

Mango Hedgehog and Marmalade

… at the market: 1 mango - preferably from South-East Asia

… at the grocery store: some sugar, if desired

dish towel - paper towels - cutting board - paring knife

Wash the mango in running water and wipe dry. Cut in half lengthwise. Remove the pit.

The first half will become the hedgehog, with a few slices of a knife and a flick of the thumb. Use the knife to cut the flesh in a checkerboard pattern, cutting deeply enough to reach the skin. Use your thumbs to push the fruit inside-out and watch the hedgehog spring to life.

Use the other half to make the marmalade. Peel it and dice the flesh. Place it in the steamer basket and cook for 10 minutes (water level 2). Throw the cooking juices away. Transfer the fruit to the blending bowl. Blend lightly (1 pulse) so as to keep some small, tender chunks.

Taste and sprinkle with a bit of sugar, if necessary.

Place the hedgehog at the center of baby's dessert plate and spoon the marmalade around it.

3 months and up · 35 mn

Cherry Clafouti

… at the market: 4.2 oz of black cherries - 1 "farm-fresh" free-range egg + 1 egg yolk - 1 pat of butter

… at the grocery store: 1.4 oz sweet butter - 2.8 oz flour - 1 oz confectioner's sugar - 2.7 fl oz. prepared milk-based pediatric nutritional supplement - 1 Tbsp flour - .2 oz cream powder - .4 oz powdered almonds - 3.3 tsp sugar

measuring glass - dishtowel - cherry pitter - 2 bowls or containers - small saucepan - mixing bowl - whisk - wooden spoon - plastic wrap - small pie pan - rolling pin - cooking rack

Take the butter out of the refrigerator and preheat the oven to 390°F (gas 6). Wash, dry and pit the cherries.

Prepare the dough. Crack the egg into the blender. Add the powdered almonds and the confectioner's sugar. Pulse 1 time. Add the softened butter and pulse again. Transfer the dough into a bowl and allow it to rest in the refrigerator.

Prepare the custard. Heat the milk in a saucepan over low heat until it simmers. In the mixing bowl, mix the egg yolk with the sugar, whisking briskly until the mixture becomes white. Add the hot milk and the cream powder. Mix well.

Put the mixture in a saucepan over low heat, stirring constantly until it thickens. Transfer to a bowl, cover with plastic wrap and set aside.

Coat the pie pan with a little butter and flour. Remove the dough from the refrigerator and roll it with the rolling pin so as to make it easier to spread in the pie pan. Pour in the custard and place the cherries on the surface. Bake for 25 min at 360° F (gas 5).

Remove from the pan as soon as you take it out of the oven and place on a rack to cool. Serve immediately.

MORE WAYS TO LOVE IT: *Almost too good to be true. Make this recipe with plums in July (5 oz), or apricots in August (5.2 oz, cut in half and pitted). Just put them on top of the cream before putting it in the oven.*

Serve with small scoop of vanilla ice cream if you like.

15 months and up — 5 mn + cooking time

Candlemas Crêpes

… at the market: 1 "farm-fresh" free-range egg

… at the grocery store: 3.5 tablespoons flour - 1 tablespoon butter - 1/3 cup prepared milk-based pediatric nutritional supplement - grape seed oil

nonstick pan (for crêpes, if possible) - small ladle - paper towel - 1 soup bowl - 1 dinner plate - dish towel

First, prepare the batter. Place the flour, milk, and butter in the blending bowl. Break the egg into it. Pulse 3 times and thin the batter with 1 tablespoon of slightly mineralized water, if necessary. There is no need to let it rest.

Pour a small amount of oil into a soup bowl. Place the pan on the stove, over low heat. Grease the hot pan with a paper towel lightly coated with oil. Pour a small ladleful of batter into the pan. Immediately roll the pan around from left to right to spread out the batter. Brown the batter for 1 minute. Turn the crepe over (flipping it in the air when you get into the swing of things) and brown the other side.

Slide it onto a plate and cover it with a clean dish towel so that it does not dry out.

Repeat these instructions for each crêpe.

MORE WAYS TO LOVE IT: *Spread blueberry or blackberry jam, quince jelly, chestnut cream or honey onto crêpes for the youngest connoisseurs.*

GOOD POINTS: *Carbohydrates in the flour, B vitamins in the yeast, a team of protein-calcium-iron-essential fatty acids in the milk, and the complete nutrition of the egg.*

MORE WAYS TO LOVE IT: *Think about adding a pinch of salt to the egg white to help it form stiff peaks. To shake things up, replace the orange blossom water with maple syrup or powdered sugar.*

15 months and up — 30 mn + 3 hr resting time

Pancakes à l'orange

… at the market: 3 "farm-fresh" free-range eggs

… at the grocery store: 3 Tbsp sugar - 2 cups sifted flour - 4 Tbsp prepared milk-based pediatric nutritional supplement - 1 oz melted butter - 7 Tbsp whipping cream - 1 teaspoon orange blossom water - 1 tiny pinch of salt - 1 small pat of butter

2 mixing bowls - whisk - electric mixer - small nonstick pan with a removable handle - wooden spatula

To prepare the batter: Start by separating 2 of the eggs. Keep the whites in a mixing bowl and save the yolks for another recipe.

Place the flour, sugar, and salt in the blending bowl. Pulse twice.

In a second mixing bowl, whisk one whole egg. Add the cream, melted butter and milk while continuing to whisk the mixture. Transfer the batter to the mixture, pulsing once between each portion of batter added.

Transfer to the mixing bowl.

Beat the egg whites (easier with an electric mixer) and gently incorporate them into the batter. Add the orange blossom water and let it rest for a good hour at room temperature.

Heat a frying pan and add a small pat of butter when it is hot. Pour in a little bit of batter (it should be roughly 4 times the thickness of a crepe).

The batter will brown and rise. Let cook for 5 min before turning it with the spatula. When both sides are golden brown (about 3 more minutes), slide the pancake onto the child's dish.

Crusty on the outside, soft and gooey on the inside.

COOKING CLUES

The Babycook Book definition of dishes…

… that can be drunk from a bottle, or eaten with a spoon:

- **Bouillon (Broccoli):** cooking juices
- **Gazpacho** (made with tomato and cucumber): cold soup made from summertime vegetables
- **Milk** (made with red or green lettuce): bouillon with a splash of milk
- **Soup:** vegetables that have been cooked and blended, with a more or less liquid consistency
- **Velouté:** smooth soup

… that can be eaten with a spoon

- **Brandade:** mix of fish and potatoes
- **Babaganoush:** savory eggplant marmalade
- **Compote:** blended cooked fruit
- **Crumble:** crunchy crust sprinkled over a fruit compote
- **Dumpling:** light leavened dough made with fish
- **Flan:** dessert made with dairy products and eggs
- **Fondue** (made with tomatoes): savory thin marmalade
- **Gnocchi:** pasta made with cheese
- **Granité:** light syrup, placed in the freezer and scraped into ice shavings with a fork
- **Gratin:** dish placed under the broiler to brown (and cook, if necessary)
- **Marmalade:** slightly blended compote that contains chunks of fruit
- **Mousse:** homogenous and fluffy consistency
- **Purée:** cooked and blended vegetable(s)
- **Stew:** vegetables that have been cooked but not blended
- **Tartare:** raw ground fish or meat with seasonings
- **Yogurt-shake:** the yogurt-based version of a milk-shake

… that can be eaten with a fork

- **Carpaccio:** thinly cut meat that is marinated and cured by the marinade
- **Meat or Fish Cake:** dish that is soft on the inside and crunchy on the outside

Cooking Clues:

- **Blanch:** place a food in a saucepan of cold water, cook until the water boils, then remove it; also used to remove tomato skins more easily: plunge the tomato into boiling water for 30 seconds and then place it in cold water
- **Brunoise:** diced vegetables
- **Crush:** cut into irregular sized pieces (= finely chop)
- **Cut:** use a knife to cut into pieces according to a specific technique (julienne or brunoise)
- **English-style:** place food in a saucepan of boiling water and then remove it
- **Fleur de sel or Flower of salt:** is made of naturally white, fine and light crystals of sea salt, rich in magnesium and iodine. It is daily hand-harvested from the surface of the ponds in the salt marshes during summer.
- **Julienne:** slice vegetables (like carrots) into thin strips the size of matchsticks
- **Moisten:** add just enough liquid to cover the food
- **Poach:** cook in a hot liquid
- **Separate:** separate the egg white and yolk
- **Set aside:** place food to the side for use later in the recipe
- **Slice:** to chop ingredients such as herbs, shallots, or onions extremely thinly with a knife or scissors
- **Stem:** remove the stems or stalks (of a fruit or vegetable)
- **Stuffing:** Any savory mix of minced ingredients
- **Sweat:** cook an ingredient for several seconds without browning, in butter or oil, while stirring
- **Thin:** add a little liquid to a mixture that is too thick
- **Thinly slice:** cut thin slices with a knife

Chef Dad's USEFUL USTENSILS

• Baking sheet • Blini pan • Bowl (or cup) • Cheese grater • Cherry pitter •
• Chinois • Cutting board • Daisy-shaped cookie cutter • Dinner plate •
• Fabric (small piece of cheesecloth, linen or jute) • Fork • Glass •
• Gratin dish (or baking dish) • Kitchen twine • Large bowl or tub •
• Mandoline • Melon baller • Mixing bowls (small and medium-sized) •
• Nonstick pan • Paper towel • Parchment paper • Paring knife • Pastry board •
• Pastry brush • Plastic containers for preserving food in freezer
• Plastic wrap • Ramekin • Saucepans (small and medium-sized) • Scissors •
• Silicon baking molds and mat • Slotted spoon • Small, clear cup •
• Small ladle • Soup bowl • Strainer • Tablespoon • Teaspoon • Toothpicks •
• Vegetable peeler • Whisk • Wooden spoon •

Also:
• Steamer basket • Plastic spatula • and a Baby Cook blender!
• Plus an apron • Dish towels • and Latex gloves for the cook •

Baby's Place Setting
• Bib with front pocket and/or long sleeves • Dessert plate and/or small cup •
• Dinner plate • Egg cup •
• Ergonomic spoon and fork that don't conduct heat and have no taste •
• High-chair or booster seat • Plastic cup • Sippy cup and lid •
•…and a bottle, until baby doesn't want it anymore !
• Soup bowl (and its saucer)

THE ABCs of recipes Babycook Book

Meal Recipes

Andalusian Gazpacho 86-87
Artichokes, Leaf by Leaf 90
Avocado Mousse "Our Way" 56-57
Babaganoush 68
Beef Stroganoff 124-125
Beet Purée 34-35
Boiled Egg and Snow Peas 84-85
Button Mushroom Purée 55
Carrot Soup 30
Cauliflower Curry in a Hurry 104-105
Cod Petals and Broccoli Buds 50
Cod Petals and Fork Smashed Zucchini 48-49
Cream of Chicken 54
Cream of Spinach 107
Crème Vichyssoise 47
Egg-cellent Caponata 80-81
Fava Bean Velouté 106
Fish Dumplings in Mushroom Sauce 128-129
Free-range Chicken Breast with Broccoli 52-53
French Mashed Potatoes 44-45
Greek yogurt and herbs 58-59
Green Asparagus Velouté 78
Ham and Pumpkin Au Gratin 135
Lentil and Dry-Cured Ham Velouté 100-101
Let's Dive into Endives 108-109
Mary Had a Little Lamb (Kefta) 118-119
Melon Ball Soup 72-73
Mini Filet of Beef and Pan Fried Potatoes 110-111
Mom and Baby: Two Peas in a Pod 74
Mom Loves you Heart and Sole 138-139
Mom's Little Ham 102
My First Artichoke... 31
My First Couscous 116-117
Pesto 63
Purée of Spring Vegetables 92-93
Purée of Summer Vegetables 94
Purée of Winter Vegetables 95
Purée of Fall Vegetables 96
Pytt-i-Panna 112-113
Pumpkin Velouté 32
Quail's Egg à la Basquaise 82-83
Red Lettuce Milk 26-27
Ricotta Gnocchi 137
Rosemary Chickpea Purée 51
Salmon Brandade with Swiss Chard 142-143
Scallop Tartare 122-123
Sea Bass with Dill 126-127
Sliced Ham, Comté, Au Jus 60-61
Socca Niçoise 132
Spinach-Mozzarella Tagliatelli Nests 64-65
Spring Velouté 77
Swedish Meatballs (Kött Bullar) 114-115
Swiss Chard Au Gratin 140-141
Thyme for Green Bean Purée 76
Tom, Tom the Turkey 134
Tomato and Goat Cheese Pasta 62
Tomato Fondue "Our Way" 69
Tomato Two Times 70
Veal Cakes 130-131
Watercress Velouté 28-29
White Bean Soup 103
Zucchini Flan-tastic 88-89

Dessert and Snack Recipes

Banana Yogurt with Honey	154
Blackcurrant Yogurt Shake	150
Candlemas Crêpes	174-175
Cherry Clafouti	172-173
Cherry Granité	106
Chocolate Chunk Cookies	168-169
Cinnamini Cookies (Pepparkakor)	166-167
Cinnamon-Apple Compote	41
Fromage Blanc with Walnuts	160
Honey-Fig Yogurt Shake	151
Langues de Chat	152-153
Madeleines	162-163
Mango Hedgehog and Marmalade	170-171
Pancakes à l'orange	176-177
Peach-Pear Compote	38
Peach-Vanilla Compote	165
Quince Compote	164
Raspberry Yogurt Shake	150
Strawberry-Banana Compote	39
Strawberry-Banana Yogurt Shake	148
Strawberry-Kiwi Yogurt Shake	149
Strawberry-Pear Compote	40
Strawberry-Rhubarb Crumble	158-159
Watermelon Granité	156-157
Yogurt Shakes à la carte	146-151

NOTES

Béaba French toll free number: 0 800 32 39 76 / www.beaba.com

The editor would like to thank:

Christophe Bougouin and Marie Claveau from Béaba, who joined us enthusiastically on the journey of creating this Chef Dad cookbook for all Babycook mothers!

Thank you to David Rathgeber for coming up with the idea of this book for Alphonse and Charlotte, and for having adapted his chef's recipes for "tiny gourmets."

Thank you to Louis, Eva, Arsène, and Arthur for their cheerfulness and sweet little faces, and to Juliette T. for kindly opening her wonderful kitchen to us.

Thank you to the talented duo Virginie Michelin and Françoise Nicol for having dreamed up and created a fun and gourmet environment for exhibiting David's recipes.

A special thank you to Jo Greeno for tiny little bear, page 177.

Thank you to Anne for her graphic design and her bright ideas!

Thank you to Laurence who, with much talent, collected and made the Chef Dad's recipes available, and thank you for giving some good pointers to young parents to help them encourage their little ones' growth and arouse their taste buds.

Thank you to Clémence for her infectiously dynamic work to gather all elements together and for having undertaken the steps necessary for our first taste-testing.

And thank you to Paule Neyrat for her precious and precise dietary advice.

Acknowledgements by Virginie Michelin:

Thank you to Hélène, my editor, for the freedom she gave me, David for his trust, Françoise for her beautiful images and those unforgettable moments that took us back to when we were children!

Thank you to Arthur, Charles, and Louis, my children, for their encouragement.

Thank you to the boutiques who graciously provided me with funding, tableware, and the objects I needed to make this book a reality.

Peintures RESSOURCE: S47 rose - Syracuse blue - Sc271 green

LILLI BULLE: 3 rue de la Forge royale - 75011 Paris - www.lillibulle.com

LA CHARRUE ET LES ETOILES: 19 rue des Francs Bourgeois - 75004 Paris

POTIRON - www.potiron.com

CONRAN SHOP - 117 rue du Bac - 75007 Paris - www.conranshop.fr

Collection Directors: Hélène Picaud and Emmanuel Jirou-Najou
Editorial Office: Isabelle Cappelli
Publishing Follow-up: Alice Gouget
Photography: Françoise Nicol
Culinary Styling: Virginie Michelin
Graphic design and DTP: Anne Chaponnay
Translation: Textra

ISBN: 978-2-84123-267-3
Printed in EC